FRIENDS WITH GUNS

Stephanie Alison Walker

BROADWAY PLAY PUBLISHING INC
New York
www.broadwayplaypub.com
info@broadwayplaypub.com

Cover art by Cece Tsou, courtesy of The Road Theatre Company

First edition: October 2022
I S B N: 978-0-88145-958-6

Book design: Marie Donovan
Page make-up: Adobe InDesign
Typeface: Palatino

FRIENDS WITH GUNS had a joint World Premiere with the following three productions.

Chapel Theatre Collective, Milwaukie, Oregon, 1-16 February 2019. The cast and creative contributors were:

SHANNON .... Danielle Weathers
JOSH .... Jason Glick
LEAH .... Claire Rigsby
DANNY .... Joseph Bertôt

Director .... Illya DeTorres
Stage Manager .... Amanda Healy
Costume design .... Elyse Grimaldi
Set design .... Illya DeTorres
Lighting/Sound design .... Dug Martell
Production Assistant .... Kate Faye Cummings
Fight choreography .... Murri Lazaroff-Babin

The Road Theatre Company in Los Angeles (Taylor Gilbert, Artistic Director/Founder; Sam Anderson, Artistic Director; Scott Alan Smith, Associate Artistic Director; Katie Witkowski, Managing Director; Darryl Johnson & Brian Graves, Technical Directors) produced by Michelle Gillette, Chet Grissom, and Susie Lever running from 15 March-12 May 2019. The cast and creative contributors were:

SHANNON .... Kate Huffman
JOSH .... Brian Graves
LEAH .... Arianna Ortiz
DANNY .... Christian Telesmar

alternate cast:
SHANNON .... Emily Jerez
JOSH .... Brian Majestic
LEAH .... Cherish Monique Duke
DANNY .... Kris Frost

Director .... Randee Trabitz
Assistant Director .... Susie Lever
Scenic Design .... Stephen Gifford
Costume Design .... Michèle Young
Lighting Design .... Derrick McDaniel
Sound Design .... David B. Marling
Props .... Heath Harper
Fight Director .... Jen Albert
Stage Manager .... Erick Marquez
Assistant Stage Manager .... Edison Logos

Uprising Theatre Company in Minneapolis, (Shannon TL Kearns, Founder & Artistic Director) running from 20 September-5 October 2019. The cast and creative contributors were:

SHANNON .... Jen Scott
LEAH .... Jess Grams
JOSH .... Tony Larkin
DANNY .... Doc Woods

Director .... Shalee Mae Coleman
Stage Manager .... Heather Burmeister
Lighting Designer .... Jake Otto
Sound design .... Claire Avitabile
Costume design .... Lisa Jones
Fight Choreographer .... Jessica Thienes

CHARACTERS & SETTING

SHANNON, *She/Her/Hers. Early 40s. Stressed-out mom to two young boys (2 & 5.) Liberal. Suffers from anxiety of the everything-needs-to-be-perfect-and-especially-I-need-to-be-perfect variety. She has a lot of fear that stops her in life. Wouldn't even know how to be begin to re-claim her power though she wants to. She's a great mom, but shackled by the expectations of what a "great mom" should be. So though she is one, she never feels like it. Realtor. Married to JOSH.*

JOSH, *He/Him/His. Early 40s, white. Liberal Democrat. Married to SHANNON. Father to their two boys. Is the main bread winner. Works a decent but boring job (data scientist at Hulu.) Has a great sense of humor. Is pretty self-aware, for the most part. Fancies himself a feminist. Knows deep down that he has an unhealthy relationship with his smart phone but would never admit that to his wife. Everybody loves him.*

LEAH, *She/Her/Hers. Early 40s, BIPOC. Wicked smart hippie/boho/punk mom to three who surfs and does yoga, is a self-proclaimed mathlete and is handy with a table saw and knitting needles. She is an empath and a connector. She's a deep eye contact kind of woman who really sees you and doesn't judge. Truly. Married to DANNY.*

DANNY, *He/Him/His. Early 40s, BIPOC. LEAH's husband and must be a different race than LEAH. Exudes a laid-back charisma that is ingrained in his DNA. This man was just born that way. He is a former shortstop for the Toronto Blue*

Jays. Grew up in Montana. Owns his own old-fashioned printing press. Distills his own whiskey. Fly fishes. And can really rock a pair of jeans and a t-shirt. He is cool and it comes easy. He is not trying, NOT ever trying to be cool. He just is. Some people might wrongly assume he's a hipster. He's not a hipster. Don't ever call him that. He's pre-hipster. He's DANNY.

Los Angeles, 2019

AUTHOR'S NOTE:

Hi. You might/probably/most definitely will find yourself being "triggered" by this play. It's that way by design. Whether you identify as anti-gun or pro-gun, you very well might/probably/most definitely will find yourself feeling uncomfortable/confronted at least once or twice during the play. I have an invitation for you: when that happens, when you find the play getting to you, I invite you to investigate what might be at the source of this reaction. Dig deep. See if there is something underneath it you've never before seen.

For me, writing this play took a tremendous amount of fear-facing, deep digging and confronting my upset and rage. I found that at the heart of my activation was the utter lack of control I felt around the issue of guns. And not just around guns, but, like, everything in the world right now. At a primal level. If you're anything like me, you want to at least feel in control of the world around you and you don't. We can't. It's utterly impossible to feel anything resembling control or stability when every day 100 Americans are killed with guns. We so desperately want to feel in control, because the alternative is helplessness and that feeling is just too difficult to live in. So instead we give ourselves over to rage. Outrage. Righteous indignation. Because at least it feels like we're doing something. We're engaged. We're enraged. And I get it.

What I discovered through writing this play, is that my own personal outrage was actually serving as a tonic to that feeling of helplessness. It was medicinal. But the side-effects were taking a toll and after a while, the tonic's healing properties stopped working on me. So, I did what I do when I'm facing something I don't understand either about myself or the world around me- I write a play. I wrote FRIENDS WITH GUNS because I grew tired of the outrage—my own and everyone else's. I tired of the outrage. I tired of the yelling. I tired of nobody listening. I thought maybe it was time for me to listen. I set down my righteousness and I stepped into this play. Into the unknown. Into my fear. I stepped into it with a commitment to leave all of my strongly held beliefs at the door. And believe me, it was terrifying. But I did it. And you can too. No matter where you stand—for guns, against guns, somewhere in the middle—you can set down the outrage and listen to the other side. Even just for the duration of this play. That's my invitation. As Leah suggests to Shannon, "Set the fear down. You can pick it up when we leave."

ACT ONE

1. The Park

(Lights up on a visibly sleep-deprived woman [SHANNON] in pajama pants, a hoodie and Birkenstocks. She clasps her large coffee cup with both hands as though it's the only thing keeping her erect. She stands downstage center and watches her kids play on the playground. Behind her is an empty bench.)

SHANNON: I do. I see you, baby. Wheeeee! Yay! You did it! You went down the slide! *(She claps as best she can while still holding her coffee. Beat)* Okay, Mommy's just gonna sit and drink her coffee and try to be human. *(She takes a step back towards the bench.)* I'm not leaving you. Just gonna sit right there. On that bench. See? *(Beat)* You're not alone, Bear. You're with Hugo. Hugo, help your brother. Please. Play with him so that Mommy can sit. Please? *(She watches. A beat. Maybe she falls a sleep for a second standing up. She takes a tentative step back towards the bench. She doesn't dare take her eyes off the kids. Another step back. She's so close to that bench, she can feel it.)* HUGO, NO! *(She rushes forward again.)* You okay, Bear? Hugo, you have to keep your brother's body safe, okay? Hugo. Hugo. HUGO! *(Quick change to forced sweet mom voice to try to cover for having just yelled)* Did you hear Mommy? Just keep him safe, please. Okay? Okay. Have fun! Safely. I'm just gonna sit and drink my coffee because it is soooo early and I'm sooo tired because someone kept Mommy

up all night last night. Again. Okay. *(She takes a step
back towards the bench.)* Yes, you can jump. Jump, yes!
(Scary Mom voice) NO! NOT on each other! *(Effort to
switch tone back to sweet Mom voice)* Not on each other.
Oh, you have a stick now! And you're pretending it's
a gun. I see that. Yes. Please put it down. Over there
in that trash can. No sticks or guns or stick guns on
the playground. Thank you! Thank you, Hugo. *(So
surprised and moved that he actually listened. This is a
win for her and she lets it in.)* You really listened. Thank
you. *(Beat)* And now your finger is the gun. Of course.
(Stressed voice breaks through) No, don't throw the—
Bear. Bear, don't throw…we keep the sand low. Low.
Okay? *(Big smile for her boys. She lustfully eyes the bench.)*
No. Not now. I can't chase you now. I'm just too tired.
You two play with each other. Please. Please. I beg you.
I beg you. I'm BEGGING you. Please! Help Mommy.
Help Mommy by playing with each other. You can do
this. *(Beat)* No. No. Because. I already answered why.
Honey. Please. Asked and answered. You can keep
asking, but you have my answer. *(Idea!)* Mommy's
going into her mommy bubble now, guys. I'm going
to keep watching you, but I'll be in my bubble, okay?
I'm in my mommy bubble now. You know what that
means. *(She watches…goes to her quiet place in her head.
It gets ruined by one of her boys needing her.)* Mommy
bubble, remember! Work it out. Be problem solvers.
Solve the…uh huh. Oh good. I'm just gonna… *(She
dares to take two big steps towards the bench. She's almost
there. So close. Just one more step. She sits. HALLELUJAH!
It is heaven. It is pure bliss. It's everything. She dares to
savor it. She even closes her eyes. When she opens them,
she sees something on the playground that launches her off
the bench.)* STOP IT! STOP IT STOP IT STOP IT STOP
IT STOP IT!!!!!! Why is it so hard?! You never listen
to me! Never! Never! Never! *(She is full blown temper
tantrum. Now that she's gone there, she has nothing to lose.*

It feels good to rage.) What's the rule?! What's the rule?!
YOU KNOW THE RULE! You have nothing to say?!
Nothing?! Don't ignore me! WHAT IS THE MOTHER
FUCKING RULE?! I know you know the rule! *(Beat.
Tries so hard to pull it back)* Yes, you did, Hugo. I just
watched you. I just watched you throw sand at your
brother's eyes. No he did not tell you to do that. Don't
even. Bear, did you want your brother to throw sand
in your eyes?! NO! And how did that make you feel?!
Hugo, it doesn't matter if you missed. The point is
that you were aiming for his eyes and you could have
gotten sand in them! No, I do not need to calm down.
YOU NEED TO LISTEN! *(She jumps and stomps.)* All I
want is to just sit on this stupid bench for more than
thirty seconds! Can you let me do that? Let me sit for
just one fucking minute?! I know I shouldn't swear!
Don't tell me what to do! You're not the boss of me.
(Full-on deep and scary momster voice) I'M THE BOSS OF
YOU!

*(Just then a woman wearing a flowy bohemian dress and
wearing a baby enters. This is* LEAH. SHANNON *sees
her standing there and looking at her and is immediately
mortified. [*LEAH *is always bouncing/swaying a bit. It's a
habit and she'll sometimes find herself doing it even when
she's not holding/wearing the baby.])*

LEAH: Hi.

SHANNON: Oh my god.

LEAH: Looks like I'm not the only one having a total
shit morning.

SHANNON: Oh my god.

LEAH: Those two—they're twins by the way.
Threenagers. Jasper and Jane. They were up at five
smearing poop on the bedroom wall. Jane's potty
trained, but Jasper's not. And he likes to play with
his fucking shit. It's a fun surprise first thing in

the morning. Not that I'm trying to one-up you or anything. And this one…going through a phase where she only sleeps in the carrier. So here we are. Six fucking AM at the park. Can't tell you how relieved I'm not the only one.

SHANNON: I am so…I'm so…

LEAH: Don't say/ embarrassed.

SHANNON: /Embarrassed.

LEAH: Happens to all of us. You just have the misfortune to have your adult tantrum witnessed by a total stranger.

LEAH laughs. It's immediately endearing.

SHANNON: Ohmygod.

LEAH: But luckily I'm not an asshole. And I don't judge. Because believe me…I've been there.

SHANNON: I'm just gonna… *(To the kids)* Kids!

LEAH: Please don't go.

SHANNON: Busy day and—

LEAH: Please. Look- our kids are so happy to be playing together. And I'm in desperate need of adult conversation. Desperate. You think you're the only mom who's ever screamed at her kids?

SHANNON: I lost it. I really lost it. And you saw that. I'm a lunatic. I'm a complete mad, raving fucking lunatic. *(To the kids)* Mommy's sorry for yelling, boys! I'm sorry for losing my temper. Mommy will take a deep breath next time.

LEAH: We all have our moments.

SHANNON: I'm a good mom. Normally. I don't usually do that…at least not in public. I could always be better and I'm always so tired but I'm a good mom. I am.

LEAH: Don't you hate justifying your parenting to a complete stranger? I'm not judging you.

SHANNON: I would if I were you.

LEAH: It's bullshit. I won't do that to another mother. Putting on a show for each other? It's oppressive. It's anti-feminist. I don't know you. Never met you. But we're sisters. If we don't have each other's backs, who will? I know how hard it is. This shit is hard. We live in LA. Surrounded by people but sometimes I feel so incredibly alone and isolated. Like there isn't another soul on this planet who understands me. In this huge city all smooshed together, but all alone. Raising the future generation side-by-side but totally alone. Right? I mean. And we're so far from family.

SHANNON: Us too. Mine's in Illinois.

LEAH: Mine's in Montana. We don't have family to back us up.

SHANNON: We don't either. I mean, my sister-in-law lives in Orange County, but she's super conservative and like a total ice queen and so judgmental and passive aggressive and the list goes on, so no thank you. I don't need that kind of help.

LEAH: No one needs that kind of help. Okay, you sit. Go ahead. I'll take the first shift. I'll keep an eye on our kiddos, make sure they don't blind each other while you sit.

SHANNON: You've got the baby...

LEAH: She sleeps better when I'm standing.

(SHANNON *looks longingly at the bench.*)

SHANNON: I usually play with them. When we come here. All those parents just staring at their phones while the kids play? That's not me. I'm out there with them crawling, climbing, jumping, chasing.

LEAH: Sit.

SHANNON: They expect me to play with them. But today. I just...I just...

LEAH: It's okay.

SHANNON: I love being a mom. I love it, I do.

LEAH: That goes without saying. But we need to give ourselves permission to admit just how hard and lonely and frustrating it can be. It's really hard.

(SHANNON *cries.*)

SHANNON: I'm sorry. I don't...

LEAH: Do not apologize for crying. Let it out. You gotta let it out.

SHANNON: Okay.

LEAH: Crying is good. I cry at least once a day. And if I haven't cried in a while, I meditate on really sad things until I cry.

SHANNON: You do?

LEAH: Oh yeah. I'll just sit there and think about cancer. Or global warming. The glaciers receding. The dry, cracked earth, the sick fish, the opioid epidemic, homelessness, people who don't even have clean water, the girls who were kidnapped by Boko Haram, the children separated from their parents at the border, SIDS, Alzheimer's, Fascism, *The Handmaid's Tale*, gerrymandering, *THE BEES!*
Sometimes I think about my death. I imagine what it would be like if I died young in a tragic and sudden accident. I think about how sad and lost my kids would be. I think about my husband who never cries and how he won't be able to stop. I think about it and I see them all stuck in this universe of pain and how I won't be here to make them feel better and...

SHANNON: That's really sad.

LEAH: *(Crying)* I fucking know.

(SHANNON *pulls the baby wipes out of her bag and offers one to* LEAH. *They wipe their tears, blow their noses. Beat)*

SHANNON: I get so mad at myself when I yell at them. And did you see them? They were just staring at me like I'm a lunatic. And I am. One second I'm the sweetest mom in the world, the next I'm—

LEAH: A toddler.

(This makes SHANNON *laugh.)*

SHANNON: I was gonna say monster.

LEAH: Look, you don't spank them do you?

SHANNON: Fuck no.

LEAH: You keep them safe, you don't wail on them…so you blow your top from time to time.

SHANNON: But I really wish I didn't.

LEAH: Yesterday I called my three-year-old daughter "fuck face." To her face. Actually, it was, "You're a fucking fuck face!" And I was kind of screaming it.

(SHANNON laughs.)

LEAH: Yeah. You're not alone, my friend.

SHANNON cries again. Relief.

LEAH: Why don't we both sit?

SHANNON: Okay.

(LEAH takes SHANNON's hand. They step backwards towards the bench.)

LEAH: On the count of three?

SHANNON: One.

LEAH: Two.

SHANNON/LEAH: Three.

(SHANNON *and* LEAH *sit. They look at each other and smile.*
They exhale.)

LEAH: I'm Leah.

SHANNON: Shannon.

LEAH: Nice to meet you, Shannon.

(End of scene)

2. Dinner Party

(LEAH *and* DANNY'*s outdoor dining area. The charming*
patio is illuminated with string lights. SHANNON, JOSH,
LEAH *and* DANNY *sit at the dining table laughing while*
DANNY *holds court with his story. There is a baby monitor*
on the table that LEAH *will glance at a couple of times in the*
scene to make sure the baby is still sleeping.)

DANNY: And she's Scottish, our doula. She's saying to
me, "Danny, ye need ta look. Th' heed ez comin' oot!
Danny! Th' heed," she says. "Th' heed! Ez comin' oot!"

(They all laugh hysterically at his Scottish accent. DANNY'*s*
natural charm is intoxicating.)

DANNY: And I had friends warn me against this.
"Whatever you do, don't look, man. It changes the way
you see your wife forever."

SHANNON: Oh, come on.

DANNY: Seriously. And one dude tells me, "You can't
un-see that horror show, man." And even Leah didn't
want me to look—

LEAH: Nooo.

SHANNON: Really?

DANNY: She didn't want me to look. But our doula just
keeps at me, "Danny! Ez brreeyant. Come an' hae a
look! Ye need tae see th' heed!"

(They laugh and laugh.)

SHANNON: You're really good at that. Hilarious.

JOSH: So, did you look?

DANNY: Of course I fucking looked. I have to look. This is life. This is childbirth. I have to look. Am I right?

JOSH: Absolutely.

DANNY: But first I ask Leah- to be a gentleman, you know- and she screams in my face to stop asking her questions.

LEAH: I was trying to push a baby out!

DANNY: So I look and I see it and I've never felt more love in my life. I mean—yeah, there's a head - or a "heed" - coming out of my best friend and that's crazy. Crazy! But it's so beautiful and I look at Leah and she's so strong and beautiful and I can't help myself, I just loudly exclaim— "You have never been so sexy!"

(They all laugh.)

DANNY: And everyone laughed.

LEAH: It was funny.

DANNY: Leah's laughing and laughing and—

LEAH: I was laughing so hard I couldn't push.

DANNY: So the doula is telling her to stop laughing: "Ye need tae quit laughin'!"

LEAH: Which makes me laugh even more.

DANNY: "Ye need tae gonnae-no laughin'!"

LEAH: It was so funny. I don't know how I was able to finally stop laughing to push him out.

DANNY: But you did. And then you did it again sixteen minutes later.

SHANNON: I can't even imagine.

DANNY: Twins, man.

LEAH: Are you guys cold? It's really cooled off.

SHANNON: I'm okay.

LEAH: Honey, will you…

DANNY: Absolutely. We have blankets, we have hats.

SHANNON: Well, if you're already up. I'll take a blanket. Thanks, Danny.

DANNY: Josh?

JOSH: Nah, I'm good.

DANNY: You look a little cold, Josh.

JOSH: Well, okay. Sure.

DANNY: All right. I'll grab the blankets and check on the kids.

LEAH: One for me too, please.

DANNY: I was gonna get you one, babe. The best one for you. You're getting the cashmere blanket, my Queen.

LEAH: Thank you, baby.

(DANNY *gives* LEAH *a romantic kiss. On the inside of her wrist, on her neck—doesn't matter—only that we see the true love and romance between these two. his affection leaves her a little starry after he exits into the house. Maybe* JOSH *pulls* SHANNON *a little closer.)*

SHANNON: It's really so lovely out here. Like a little vacation. I showed this house a few times, you know.

LEAH: Did you?

JOSH: It should've been your listing.

SHANNON: *(Giving him a "not now" look)* Babe.

JOSH: It's true.

SHANNON: Anyway, I thought for sure one of my clients was going to make an offer, but they ended up buying something through an another agent. That was fun.

LEAH: Really? Does that happen a lot?

JOSH: It's a cutthroat business.

SHANNON: I always felt this was one of the selling points of the house. The indoor/outdoor California vibe. It has good flow.

LEAH: Yes. I'm all about flow.

JOSH: Totally. Here's to ordinary differential equations.

(JOSH *raises his glass.* LEAH *laughs.*)

SHANNON: Is that a math joke?

JOSH: Flow. You didn't get that?

LEAH: I got it. Fellow math geek.

JOSH: Oh yeah? I'm totally hot for math.

(SHANNON *practically spits out her drink.*)

SHANNON: That should be on a T-shirt.

JOSH: Now you know what to get me for Father's Day.

LEAH: I'd buy that shirt. And wear it proudly.

(DANNY *returns with the blankets and wearing a hand knit pussy hat.*)

DANNY: I feel warmer already!

(*They erupt in laughter.*)

JOSH: Nice hat, man.

DANNY: Got one for you too, brother.

(DANNY *tosses* JOSH *a hat.* JOSH *puts it on.*)

SHANNON: You've never looked so sexy.

DANNY: Leah made them.

SHANNON: You knit?

LEAH: A little. I used to knit a lot more.

(DANNY *hands* SHANNON *a blanket. She scoots closer to* JOSH *and shares the blanket with him. They snuggle.* DANNY *and* LEAH *snuggle under their blanket.* DANNY *produces a joint...*)

DANNY: Do you...?

SHANNON: Not since college.

JOSH: Special occasions.

LEAH: This is definitely a special occasion, no?

(DANNY *hands the joint to* LEAH.)

LEAH: I'll just pump and dump.

(LEAH *lights it and takes a hit. Then offers it to* SHANNON.)

JOSH: It's not every day you make new friends.

(SHANNON *takes the joint.*)

SHANNON: Okay, sure, why not?

(SHANNON *takes a delicate hit and passes it to* JOSH *who takes a hit. Through the following, they pass the joint.*)

SHANNON: I'm just gonna say it out loud because I couldn't be more pleased: This is going so well.

LEAH: So well.

SHANNON: Right?! (*To* JOSH) Right, hon?

JOSH: Yes. You were right. These guys are awesome. You guys are pretty cool.

DANNY: Thanks, man.

JOSH: You're so cool, you make me feel cool by proxy.

SHANNON: You're cool on your own, baby. Not just by proxy.

DANNY: Yeah, I don't usually like most people.

LEAH: It's true.

DANNY: But I like you guys. This is good.

JOSH: I want us to all be best friends, is that weird to say?

SHANNON: Maybe you should lay off the grass just a little, sweetie.

LEAH: I think this is gonna be grand. Friday night weekly dinners where the rule is that you cannot clean your house.

JOSH: No cleaning before guests? Ha! Shannon won't be able to do that.

SHANNON: I will. I'm gonna try!

LEAH: No cleaning at all. That's the whole point. No stress.

SHANNON: What if my stress is caused by a dirty house?

LEAH: Then think of this as an experiment that will set you free.

JOSH: She can't do it.

SHANNON: Challenge accepted.

LEAH: It's about just being together.

DANNY: Community.

LEAH: Exactly!

DANNY: I like it.

SHANNON: And our date night idea where we switch off dropping the kids off with each other. One night-

LEAH: Or morning. Brunch dates are always good.

SHANNON: Oh, I love brunch. Waffles. *(She imagines waffles)* Mmmmm... *(Then)* I'm stoned. Whoa.

DANNY: That's adorable.

(The joint comes back around to SHANNON *and she just stares at it.* JOSH *takes it.)*

LEAH: This is gonna be great. We'll save so much money on babysitting and actually reinstate date night.

SHANNON: Ah, date night.

LEAH: And the kids will just love being together.

SHANNON: I love that we have the same parenting philosophy. Because that's a total deal breaker between friends.

LEAH: I hear you.

DANNY: What a relief. So you guys spank your kids too?

LEAH: That's not funny, Danny.

DANNY: It's kind of funny.

JOSH: *(To* SHANNON*)* He's joking, Shan.

SHANNON: I know.

LEAH: Terrible joke.

DANNY: Funny joke.

SHANNON: *(To herself)* Philosophy. Phisopholy. Phil-o-so-phy.

*(*JOSH *looks at* SHANNON.*)*

JOSH: You okay?

SHANNON: Yesiree.

LEAH: She's stoned. It's adorable.

DANNY: You like baseball, Josh?

JOSH: Lifelong Twins fan.

LEAH: Danny's real modest so he won't tell you, but I will.

DANNY: Leah…

JOSH: What?

LEAH: Danny played shortstop for the Toronto Blue Jays.

JOSH: WHAT?

DANNY: Only one season. Right out of college. It was no big deal.

JOSH: That's…okay, you own your own printing press, you distill your own whiskey, you run marathons and you're a former Major League ball player?!

SHANNON: Wow.

JOSH: I'm not jealous.

DANNY: We should go to a Dodgers game. You want to meet Kershaw?

JOSH: I'm sorry…what?

DANNY: Clayton Kershaw?

JOSH: Yeah, I'm familiar.

DANNY: Little known fact: Kershaw's great uncle discovered Pluto.

SHANNON: I have no idea who they're talking about.

LEAH: Pitcher for the Dodgers.

JOSH: So you're friends or…

DANNY: Friends of friends. I can introduce you. If you want. No pressure.

JOSH: Uh… Yeah.

DANNY: Cool.

JOSH: Cool.

(JOSH *is very impressed and a little starstruck by* DANNY.)

LEAH: The kids are too quiet.

SHANNON: I was just thinking the same thing.

DANNY: It's the NyQuil. Put some in their water. Works like a charm.

(They laugh.)

DANNY: I put a movie on for them. They're fine.

LEAH: Is a movie okay?

JOSH: We try not to poison their minds with media - we don't have a TV in our house and no ipads or anything like that, but—

DANNY: Okay cool. They're watching *Texas Chainsaw Massacre*. Seem to really love it.

JOSH guffaws.

LEAH: Danny! *(To JOSH)* He's kidding.

DANNY: He knows.

SHANNON: So's Josh. We have a TV. We poison their minds with media.

DANNY: What a relief.

JOSH: You guys have plans for Labor Day?

LEAH: Labor Day?

JOSH: Yeah.

LEAH: Uh…Nothing planned yet. Seeing as it's only May.

JOSH: We should do something. Like all go to a park and picnic. Let the kids play in the trees all day somewhere in Topanga or something.

LEAH: I am in love with that idea.

DANNY: Love it. Let's do it!

SHANNON: *(Teary eyed)* I am so happy you moved into our neighborhood. *(Getting emotional)* I'm so happy we met.

LEAH: Me too.

JOSH: A little weed just opens up the flood gates.

SHANNON: I'm fine, Joshy.

DANNY: She's fine, Joshy.

SHANNON: I'm just so excited. *(To* JOSH*)* I mean, I told you, didn't I?

JOSH: Yeah. You did. And I was hoping you were right. I mean you were already planning our lives together. Lot of pressure.

DANNY: Oh yeah. On this side too. Leah went on and on about you too, Shannon.

SHANNON: Really?

LEAH: Of course, Mama.

DANNY: I mean, you could've turned out to be science deniers or some bullshit like that.

JOSH: Or Trump voters.

SHANNON: Oh my god!

LEAH: Fuck no.

JOSH: You could've been gun people.

SHANNON: Just stop.

JOSH: I mean...

SHANNON: That would be ridiculous.

JOSH: Fucking guns.

SHANNON: Hate 'em.

JOSH: After this last one, I say take 'em all away.

SHANNON: Oh my god, this last one.

JOSH: It's the only answer. It's gone too far. I mean, we're just supposed have an escape plan for any time we're in public now because some deranged, sociopathic motherfucker with an AR-15 might decide to shoot up a crowd? That's no fucking way to live. Take 'em away. Take 'em all away.

(Silence. LEAH *and* DANNY *exchange a look.)*

JOSH: Sorry...that kind of brought down the festive mood. Sorry.

SHANNON: Yeah, not really the best dinner party conversation, babe.

JOSH: Says the woman who told her Scabies story at a dinner at my boss' house.

SHANNON: Okay, yeah. That was bad.

LEAH: Scabies?

DANNY: So, you're a "take 'em all away" kind of guy?

LEAH: Danny.

JOSH: Best way to stop a bad guy with a gun is to take away his gun.

DANNY: You realize there are more guns than people in this country.

JOSH: I do.

SHANNON: Is that true?

DANNY: Approximately three-hundred-and-fifty-seven million guns. Take 'em all away? How?

JOSH: We have to at least try. We owe that to the victims.

SHANNON: I just read this statistic that more people in our country are killed by toddlers with guns than terrorists. How scary is that?

DANNY: Don't you think that statistic says more about the low number of terrorist attacks than it does about guns?

SHANNON: What?

DANNY: The point you were trying to make was about—

LEAH: *(Warning)* Danny.

DANNY: About guns being bad, yes? More toddlers kill people with guns than terrorists. Should it be the other way around? Would you prefer more deaths by terrorists than by toddlers with guns?

SHANNON: Um…well, of course I don't—

JOSH: How about no toddlers with guns? I think that's her point.

SHANNON: My point—

DANNY: Your point is guns are bad.

SHANNON: Yes. That's my point.

(There's another beat)

LEAH: What movie did you say the kids are watching, Danny?

DANNY: A gun is a tool. It's a machine. Machines aren't moral or immoral. They aren't capable of choice. They're metal and plastic. They aren't good or bad. They just are.

LEAH: Danny.

DANNY: No, if we're gonna be each other's "tribe", they should know. They should know we have guns.

(JOSH laughs. No one else does. It gets real quiet.)

SHANNON: *(To JOSH)* I don't think he's joking this time.

(JOSH suddenly stands.)

JOSH: You have guns?! Our kids are alone in the next room and you have guns in your house?!

LEAH: Not in the house. They're in the garage in a safe.

DANNY: Locked up. Kids don't even know we have guns. We don't take them out around them.

LEAH: They're in a safe within a safe in the garage.

DANNY: Except for the one I have holstered.

(WHAT. THE. FUCK?!)

LEAH: Danny.

DANNY: That was a joke.

LEAH: Jesus. Seriously.

SHANNON: You have guns in your home and you didn't tell me?

JOSH: *(To* SHANNON*)* You didn't ask?

SHANNON: It didn't even occur to me. I never ever would have in a million years thought—

JOSH: You're supposed to ask. No matter what. You're supposed to ask.

SHANNON: I just...I just assumed.

JOSH: You assumed, Shannon? Why? Because she does yoga?

SHANNON: I, I—

JOSH: Because she smells like patchouli?!

LEAH: It's sandalwood, actually.

JOSH: What?

LEAH: Sandalwood.
Let's just all take a breath—

SHANNON: I never would have thought in a million years that you guys had guns in your home. You're liberals!

JOSH: We agreed to never assume.

LEAH: Breathe in and out—

JOSH: Damn it. We were gonna go to Topanga with you guys!

DANNY: Who says we can't go to Topanga now?

JOSH: I'm not...I mean.. Guns. No.

LEAH: You're freaking out.

JOSH: Yeah. Yeah.

SHANNON: I mean...I mean...we just...we're not...

LEAH: We're not crazy gun nuts or anything like that.
We're responsible gun owners.
I grew up with them. I'm all for appropriate gun
control. I am. I'm for common sense gun laws. And
also I support the second amendment.

DANNY: Don't apologize.

LEAH: I'm not.

JOSH: What kind of guns? How many? For what
purpose?

DANNY: For what purpose? For the purpose of
exercising our constitutional right.

JOSH: Why would parents of young kids need a safe
filled with guns in their home in West Los Angeles?!

DANNY: I don't like your tone.

LEAH: We have a couple of rifles for hunting and skeet
shooting, we have a few different pistols that we take
to the indoor range for target practice and Danny has
his collection of antique long guns...

DANNY: My favorite is my Springfield Model 1855
Musket.

LEAH: And...

SHANNON: You hunt?

LEAH: Danny used to. In Montana.

JOSH: And? You said "And." Are there more?

(Beat)

DANNY: I have an AR-15.

JOSH: You have an AR-15?!

DANNY: Here we go. This'll be fun.

JOSH: A fucking assault rifle?!

DANNY: Yep. There it is.

LEAH: "AR" doesn't stand for "Assault Rifle". That's a common misconception.

SHANNON: What does it stand for?

LEAH: Armalite Rifle. Armalite was the company that first made them.

DANNY: The AR-15 is not an assault rifle. Assault rifles are fully automatic. AR-15s are not.

JOSH: Why on earth would you even need one?

DANNY: It's not about need.

JOSH: And and and how do you even have one? Aren't they illegal in California?

DANNY: I built it.

JOSH: You built it.

DANNY: Bought the parts and custom built it.

LEAH: He likes to build things.

JOSH: So build a table, then. Not a weapon of mass destruction!

LEAH: He actually built this table.

SHANNON: It's a really nice table.

DANNY: Thank you.

JOSH: How many guns exactly do you own?

DANNY: Ten. (*Quick beat*) No eleven.

SHANNON: Eleven?

JOSH: I don't even know what the fuck…

DANNY: You're surprised we have guns, I'm surprised you don't.

JOSH: Why?

DANNY: Because I think everyone should.

JOSH: Why?

DANNY: Because they're awesome.

JOSH: Because they're awesome? I think it's time to go.

LEAH: Danny, don't be a dick.

DANNY: I won't be judged in my own home. I won't be judged.

JOSH: *(To* SHANNON*)* Let's get the kids and let's get out of here.

(SHANNON *doesn't move. She's conflicted.)*

SHANNON: What if we just take a breath and…and… listen to Danny and Leah explain or…

JOSH: No.

LEAH: Would it help if we showed you the safe so that you could see for yourself?

JOSH: Nope.

SHANNON: Maybe.

LEAH: They're not loaded. We store the ammunition separate from the guns.

JOSH: We're gonna take a pass.

LEAH: Are you sure?

JOSH: Hard fucking pass.

SHANNON: I'm sorry. It's late. We should really get the kids to bed.

LEAH: Please don't let this come between us. There's no reason—

DANNY: It's no use with these people, Leah.

JOSH: These people?!

LEAH: He didn't mean it like that.

DANNY: This is so fucking typical.

LEAH: Danny. Shut up.

DANNY: I don't like people making assumptions about my family just because we're gun owners. And it's always the same thing as soon as our liberal friends find out. They all shun us. Fucking sheep.

JOSH: I'm not a fucking sheep.

DANNY: Why don't you try thinking for yourself and then we'll see.

JOSH: Shannon.

SHANNON: Thank you for a…lovely evening.

(As JOSH and SHANNON exit:)

LEAH: We're still on for yoga tomorrow, right?

(End of scene)

3. The Morning After

(The next morning)

(JOSH sits at the kitchen table drinking coffee. SHANNON enters in her yoga outfit.)

SHANNON: The kids are dressed and fed and are actually playing nicely in their room.

JOSH: Thanks.

SHANNON: I'll be home before you guys are back from the party.

JOSH: Where is it again?

SHANNON: Chuck E Cheese.

JOSH: No.

SHANNON: I did the last Chuck E Cheese party.

JOSH: Putting parents through this. It's hostile.

SHANNON: It's a kids birthday party, Josh. Don't be so dramatic. And it's only two hours of your life.

JOSH: I'm so hungover. I don't think I can do it.

SHANNON: Well, you have to.

JOSH: What if…Hugo's sick?

SHANNON: He's not sick.

JOSH: But what if he were sick?

SHANNON: You really want to tell Hugo he can't go to his best friend's birthday party?

JOSH: Couldn't you take this one…

SHANNON: No, Josh.

JOSH: Please? I'll make it up to you.

SHANNON: She's gonna be here any minute.

JOSH: So you're really still going to yoga with her?

SHANNON: Yes. We're going to yoga. You don't want me to be friends with her at all?

JOSH: Well…

SHANNON: Because I really like her. I like them. I had so much fun last night. I know you did too.

JOSH: Promise me you'll never let the kids go over there without you.

SHANNON: We're only two blocks apart. I could drop the kids off for a couple of hours if I had a showing. The kids get along so well.

JOSH: Promise me.

SHANNON: Not to have to hire a babysitter.

JOSH: Babe.

SHANNON: They said they're locked away in a safe in the garage.

JOSH: I can't believe you'd even consider letting our kids in a house with guns!

SHANNON: But they're not technically in the house. They're in the garage. In a locked safe. And the garage is locked.

JOSH: It's the same to me.

SHANNON: That seems like an overreaction.

JOSH: It absolutely fucking is and I don't care. I'm fine with overreacting when it comes to firearms around my kids. It's our rule. It's our family rule. The kids don't go to houses where there are guns. Ever. We agreed. Why is this hard?

SHANNON: I agree. You're right. Of course. I'm just…

JOSH: You're trying to normalize it.

SHANNON: No, I'm not.

JOSH: Yeah you are. That's exactly what you're doing. You're trying to normalize it. Your brain is. Because you want to be friends with her.

SHANNON: God, why do they have to be gun people?!

JOSH: I'm just saying maybe it would be best to end things before we get too attached.

SHANNON: I hear you. It's just…It's hard to make new friends. And it seemed like you really got along well with Danny.

JOSH: He said he'd teach me to distill whiskey.

SHANNON: And introduce you to that pitcher.

JOSH: Kershaw.

SHANNON: Dammit. They're really cool people.

JOSH: Really cool.

SHANNON: Except for the guns.

JOSH: The fucking guns.

SHANNON: It just seems intolerant of us to not be friends with people who are on the opposite side of just one issue.

JOSH: Be careful her gun doesn't go off while she's in downward dog.

SHANNON: She's not gonna bring a gun to yoga.

JOSH: How do you know?

SHANNON: First of all, isn't that illegal? And secondly, they said they keep their guns in the safe.

JOSH: You need to ask her if she has a concealed carry permit.

SHANNON: They have those in California?

JOSH: We need to get the whole picture.

SHANNON: I think you might be blowing this a bit out of proportion.

JOSH: They have an actual safe. Filled with guns. Twenty-four hour access to firearms. Plural.

SHANNON: Fine. We won't go over there anymore. We'll have them here. Or we'll meet out somewhere else. The beach. A park. Restaurants. Whatever.

JOSH: Yoga?

SHANNON: Yes. You're the one who said I needed something- a coping mechanism - to help with my anxiety.

JOSH: I know.

SHANNON: And Leah said this teacher is amazing.

JOSH: I have no interest in stopping you from going to yoga. But...

SHANNON: But what?

JOSH: I don't want to be friends with gun people, okay? No matter how cool they are. And I don't care if that makes me intolerant.

(SHANNON *gets a text alert.*)

SHANNON: Leah's here. It's just yoga, Josh.

(SHANNON *exits. End of scene*)

4. Yoga

(*In Leah's VW bus driving to yoga.*)

LEAH: Thanks.

SHANNON: For what?

LEAH: For not bailing.

SHANNON: Oh. Yeah. No. (*Beat*) Thanks for driving.

LEAH: My pleasure.

SHANNON: VW bus.

LEAH: My baby.

SHANNON: Hippie.

LEAH: Yeah.

SHANNON: Hippie with a gun. Guns. I promised myself I wouldn't bring it up.

LEAH: It's okay.

SHANNON: I just have so many questions.

LEAH: You can ask me anything. Go ahead. Shoot. See what I did there?

SHANNON: Aah…funny.

LEAH: Easy.

SHANNON: You're not a member of the NRA are you?

LEAH: No!

SHANNON: Oh, thank God.

LEAH: Fuck no. Fuck those assholes.

SHANNON: I was afraid to even ask.

LEAH: That's the assumption though, isn't it? Someone owns guns they're a card carrying NRA member?

SHANNON: Um well, yeah.

LEAH: But not true. Only six or seven percent of all gun owners in America area actually NRA members.

SHANNON: Really?

LEAH: Really.

SHANNON: Before I met you I didn't even know that liberals owned guns. I realize how stupid and naive that sounds, but...

LEAH: You're not the only one.

(Beat)

SHANNON: What's it like?

LEAH: What's what like?

SHANNON: Never mind.

LEAH: Shooting a gun?

SHANNON: Yeah. I mean. Never mind.
But yeah. Shooting...a gun. What's it...what's it like? I mean... *(She looks at LEAH.)*

LEAH: Want to find out?

SHANNON: No.

LEAH: Because there's an indoor range that I like that's not too far and, I mean, we'd have to swing by my house and pick up my gun, but—

SHANNON: So you don't keep a gun in the car?

LEAH: No. Never.

SHANNON: Oh. Okay.

LEAH: So you thought I had a gun in the car?

SHANNON: I didn't know.

LEAH: You can ask. You can always just ask.

SHANNON: Okay.

(Beat)

LEAH: So, yoga or shooting range?

SHANNON: Oh, I couldn't.

LEAH: It just seemed.

SHANNON: Curiosity.

LEAH: Sure.

SHANNON: I mean. I, I, I, I couldn't. I shouldn't. I mean.

LEAH: That's fine. I would never…

SHANNON: But…

LEAH: Yeah?

(LEAH looks at SHANNON. Long pause)

SHANNON: I'm really looking forward to the chanting. I mean I've never been to a yoga class with chanting before.

LEAH: The chanting is sublime.

SHANNON: Shit. I forgot my yoga mat.

LEAH: They have them there.

SHANNON: No, I can't. That's not me. I can't use somebody else's yoga mat.
I can never stop thinking about how many people have sweat all over them or how many people got their athlete's foot all over the mat and— Do you have an extra mat? I guess I wouldn't be so worried if I was using your mat. I know it's not cool to be a germaphobe, but it's really more about me having an

overactive imagination. I start thinking about someone drooling on the mat or sneezing on it and then I'm just a ball of anxiety which undermines the entire objective, so do you? Have an extra mat?

LEAH: You could use mine if you want and I'll use one from the studio.

SHANNON: Really?

LEAH: Of course.

SHANNON: I know I might seem like an easy going person, but I'm really not.

LEAH: Oh my god, I have got to get around this fucking douchebag!

(SHANNON *holds on while* LEAH *maneuvers. She watches* LEAH.)

SHANNON: You're, uh…

LEAH: Sorry. Little road ragey today.

SHANNON: Wouldn't have expected that.

LEAH: Well.
So. All good with the mat situation? To yoga then?

SHANNON: Yeah.

LEAH: You're gonna love it. It's weird at first. But…

SHANNON: When was your first time?

LEAH: Chanting?

SHANNON: No. Shooting a gun. I mean. How old were you?

LEAH: I was ten.

SHANNON: Ten?!

LEAH: Yep.

SHANNON: Ten years old?

LEAH: I grew up on a farm. Guns were just a part of my childhood. *(To another driver)* Texting while driving. Of course.

SHANNON: What, um, what kind of gun was it? The, the, the first one.

LEAH: Shotgun. Did you see that woman? She was driving with her phone right in front of her face.

SHANNON: Ten years old with a shotgun?

LEAH: Dad took me skeet shooting. I was a good shot. Exploded a clay pigeon right out of the sky. It was... Exhilarating. Dad was proud. I liked him being proud of me.

SHANNON: Wow.

LEAH: I was fifteen the first time I shot and killed an animal.
It was a pheasant. I cried. But then we ate it for dinner and I was proud to provide for my family.

SHANNON: My god.

LEAH: After the pheasant, Dad took me deer hunting—

SHANNON: Oh Bambi.

LEAH: I know. I watched as he fell a deer.

SHANNON: Fell?

LEAH: Shot.

SHANNON: Fell is such a gentle word to describe something so violent.

LEAH: That deer provided food for months but I couldn't get its eyes out of my mind. I decided hunting wasn't for me.

SHANNON: So you don't hunt.

LEAH: No.

SHANNON: But you still have guns.

LEAH: Yes, we do.

SHANNON: Why?

LEAH: Guns were always around so I haven't had a fear of them. Ever. I was kind of indifferent for a while, actually. Could take 'em or leave 'em. Seriously. I never owned a gun until…this thing happened. Shit!

SHANNON: What?

LEAH: *(Regarding her nipple)* I sprung a leak. My boob's leaking and my shirt is already soaked through. I gotta pull over.

(LEAH pulls over and parks.)

SHANNON: Do you need something?

LEAH: I got it. *(She reaches behind the seat and digs into her diaper bag. Pulls out a fresh breast pad. She reaches into her bra and removes the soaked one.)* It's totally soaked through.

SHANNON: Oh, I don't miss that.

(LEAH tosses the wet one into her diaper bag and she dries her shirt and breast with a spit up rag.)

LEAH: I'm away from the baby for like ten minutes and already.

SHANNON: That biological connection is something.

LEAH: Yeah, it is something. *(She shoves the dry breast pad into her bra.)* So much better.

SHANNON: So, what happened? I mean the thing. You said a thing happened…

LEAH: Right. We're gonna miss the chanting if I tell you the story.

SHANNON: That's okay.

She tells the following story like she's told it a million times before. It's well-crafted and matter-of-fact. And she knows how to grab the listener's attention with the suspense of the story.

LEAH: All right. Well, it was my twenty-fifth birthday. This was before I met Danny. I was living alone in a beautiful one-bedroom apartment in Billings. I wake up suddenly in the middle of the night with a funny feeling. Something isn't right. I sit up in bed, hyper-alert when I hear it…the jostling of the knob on my front door. It's clear, someone is trying to get through the lock.

SHANNON: Oh my god.

LEAH: I call nine-one-one and tell them someone is breaking into my apartment and they tell me to go lock myself in my bedroom and wait for them to arrive. Lock myself in my bedroom and wait. Wait for him to get in and rape me or the police to arrive and save me.

SHANNON: Oh my god.

LEAH: Yeah. I have to do more than that. So I run to my tool box and I grab a hammer. I creep up to the door, clutching my hammer and the noise stops. I don't know how, but I summon the courage to look out the peephole to see this guy. I don't want to, but I have to. What I see chills me to the bone. There isn't just one guy. There are two. They're looking at the door. They know I'm right on the other side. So, I gather my voice and pray for it to be strong. "The police are on their way," I say. And the one guy, he smiles. This horrible smile. The other goes back to working on the lock. I step back from the door and I know I have to do something. So I run through my apartment turning on lights. Then I turn the radio on and crank it really loud.
(She sings)
Gloria (Gloria)
I think they got your number (Gloria)
I think they got the alias (Gloria)

that you've been living under
It's blasting through the apartment and I'm praying it
wakes my neighbors. I'm praying it scares those two....
Those two...away. But they don't leave. They just
keep working on the lock. So I start dragging furniture
to block the door. And I'm thinking, "Where are the
police?!" I turn the music off so that I can hear them.
It's quiet. I stop reciting Hail Marys in my head and I
listen. *(Beat)* Nothing. I'm too afraid to look through
the peephole again. So I just stand there. With my
hammer. Listening. Waiting. For them to...or for the
police to save me. I have no idea how I'm going to fight
off two men with a hammer. Two men with about two
hundred pounds on me. One thing is abundantly clear:
this is not a level playing field. I am lying in wait.
I stand there waiting, listening for what feels like an
eternity until I see the red and blue lights filter through
my window. The police finally arrive a full 42 minutes
after I called. Forty-two minutes. The men were long
gone by then. They'd apparently given up on the lock.
I have to move all the furniture to let the police inside
so that they can take my statement. They leave and I
try to go back to sleep. But...of course, I can't. At 9AM,
I head to my neighborhood hardware store to buy two
bolt locks for my door. Then I go to a gun store and
I purchase a Glock19. It's my twenty-fifth birthday.
If those men ever came back, I wouldn't be standing
there with a hammer. I'd be waiting for them with my
gun.

SHANNON: Oh my god. Oh my god, Leah.

LEAH: So, yeah.

SHANNON: Holy shit. I mean. Holy fucking shit. I'm so
glad they didn't get through that lock!

LEAH: Me too.

SHANNON: Thank you for sharing that with me.

LEAH: Yeah, no.

SHANNON: That is like—everything you shared- it's like the exact thing I've been scared of my whole life. Someone breaking in and…I really mean it. It's my nightmare. Second to being jumped on the street, dragged into an alley and raped. Or raped by someone I know. Or waking up with a stranger on top of me which is exactly what happened to my college roommate.

LEAH: Yeah. So that's why. For me. I mean, I'm not sure I'd go so far as to call it an "equalizer," but it's somewhere in that neighborhood.

SHANNON: Overalls.

LEAH: What?

SHANNON: I've always loved overalls and wanted to wear them but I took this self-defense class in high school and was told not to ever wear clothing that would be easy for an attacker to cut-away like overalls. So I never wore them. Even though I really wanted to. That sounds really stupid. I'm sorry. I don't know what made me think of that.

LEAH: We're taught to do a lot of things to make sure we don't end up victims— the way we walk—

SHANNON: Never make eye contact and if you do, don't look down afterwards. Look over. Or up and away. But never down.

LEAH: Never walk home alone.

SHANNON: Never walk anywhere alone at night.

LEAH: Don't get too drunk.

SHANNON: Don't ever let your drink out of your sight.

LEAH: Always check underneath your car before getting into it.

SHANNON: And the backseat.

LEAH: Lock your doors as soon as you get into the car.

SHANNON: Don't go running alone at night.

LEAH: Or you're definitely asking to be raped. May as well wear a sign.

SHANNON: Never forget to be afraid.

LEAH: All the time.

SHANNON: I'm sick of it. I'm tired of being afraid all the time. Sometimes…when I pass by a driving range I fantasize about going in and—

LEAH: You mean shooting range?

SHANNON: What did I say?

LEAH: Driving range. That's golf. Never mind.

SHANNON: Oh, that's funny. No, I meant shooting range.

LEAH: You fantasize about going in…?

SHANNON: And holding a gun, pointing it at a target and pulling the trigger.
But I was afraid of that too. *(Beat)* I want to feel what it feels like to be the one with the power. For once.

5. The Range

(We hear a loud and jarring BANG. Then another. Beat. BANG. Beat. BANG. Beat. BANG.)

(SHANNON and LEAH cross to downstage center and put on "ears & eyes" [ear and eye protection]. LEAH holds a 357 Magnum Smith & Wesson revolver and demonstrates how to hold it. SHANNON's arms are folded tightly across her chest. With every BANG, SHANNON involuntarily jumps.)

SHANNON: *(Yelling over the noise of the gunfire)* I can't stop jumping!

LEAH: You'll get used to it.

(BANG! SHANNON *jumps again.)*

(Between the "ears" muffling the sound and the noise of the other people at the range shooting, LEAH *and* SHANNON *have to yell to be heard.)*

LEAH: This is heavier than it looks. The recoil on this one isn't bad, but you'll still feel it. Keep a firm grip. Feet shoulder width apart and knees slightly bent. Lock the hammer like this. Line up the sites, gently squeeze the trigger, and the gun goes off. Okay? You wanna look through here and focus down at the target. And never point a gun at something you don't intend to shoot. Obvious. But you'd be surprised how many idiots accidentally shoot themselves at the range.

*(*SHANNON *laughs nervously then looks around.)*

LEAH: Just keep it pointed down range. I'm gonna hand it to you in a second here, but first I'm gonna show you: it's not loaded.

*(*LEAH *opens the cylinder and shows* SHANNON.*)*

LEAH: See? Cylinder's empty.

*(*LEAH *closes the cylinder and hands the gun to* SHANNON. SHANNON *takes it and keeps it pointed down.)*

SHANNON: It's heavy.

LEAH: Yep.

SHANNON: Am I holding it right?

LEAH: Choke up on it a bit.

*(*LEAH *helps* SHANNON *adjust the grip.)*

LEAH: Good. You wanna line up your sites and point it down range at your target.

(SHANNON *slowly raises the gun and points it at the target.*)

SHANNON: Like this?

LEAH: Yeah. Here. Let me…

(LEAH *reaches around* SHANNON'*s body and helps her hold the gun…she adjusts her aim a bit.*)

LEAH: You could widen your stance a bit.

(SHANNON *does.*)

LEAH: Don't forget to bend your knees.
Good. Ready? First the hammer, then the trigger.

(SHANNON *just stands there holding the gun.*)

LEAH: Whenever you're ready.

(SHANNON *is frozen.*)

LEAH: Go ahead and squeeze. It's not loaded, remember.

(SHANNON *does. She immediately winces and looks away.*)

SHANNON: Oh my god oh my god.

LEAH: Good.

SHANNON: I did it.

LEAH: Yep. Let's load her up.

(SHANNON *places the gun down on the shelf in front of her. She steps back so that* LEAH *can step in.* LEAH *loads the gun.* SHANNON *watches.*)

LEAH: See, you just open the cylinder and put the bullets in the holes.

(LEAH *finishes loading the gun, closes the cylinder and offers it to* SHANNON.)

(SHANNON *doesn't take it. Instead she looks at her hands.*)

SHANNON: I'm shaking. (*She breathes to try to calm herself.*)

LEAH: It's not a monster. It's a gun. It only does what you tell it to do.

(SHANNON *is terrified.*)

SHANNON: My hands are sweating. (*She wipes her hands on her pants. She shakes her hands out. She puts her hands on her knees and breathes. She looks at* LEAH.)

LEAH: It's the same gun you just held.

SHANNON: Except now it's loaded.

LEAH: Yep. It's good to remember that.

SHANNON: I can't believe I'm doing this.

LEAH: Set the fear down. You can pick it back up when we leave.

SHANNON: It's not a monster.

LEAH: Nope. It's just a gun. You ready to tell it what to do?

(LEAH *offers the gun again.* SHANNON *takes it. She keeps the gun pointed down as she adjusts her grip and makes sure she has it right.* LEAH *stands behind* SHANNON.)

(SHANNON *raises the gun slowly and lines the sites up with the target. She exhales. She closes her eyes for a beat and then opens them with determination.*)

LEAH: Whenever you're ready.

SHANNON: All right. Here I go. (*She prepares to pull the trigger. She lowers the hammer then squeezes the trigger. She flinches and then winces as the fire bursts out of the end of the gun. Everything about this moment surprises her.*) Holy crap!

LEAH: You okay?

SHANNON: Did you see the flames?

LEAH: I did.

SHANNON: Holy shit. This is crazy.

LEAH: Try again.

SHANNON: I wanna try again.

LEAH: Do it. Confidence. You got this. Do it. Do it. *(She pulls the trigger again.)* Damn. Not bad! You're right on target.

(SHANNON fires another slightly less hesitant shot. She wipes her sweat off her palms and steadies herself.)

LEAH: You got this.

(All the rage that has been buried SHANNON's whole life rises up and flies out of her body, traveling at the speed of a bullet towards the target where it explodes. She breathes in, then out, fires again. BANG. Beat. BANG. Beat. BANG. Until all six bullets are spent.)

(She puts the gun down. She looks calm, centered. Triumphant)

(LEAH is jumping up and down with excitement behind her.)

LEAH: Wooo hoo! That was AMAZING!

(Tears stream down SHANNON's face. She removes the protective glasses, wipes the tears out of her eyes and gives LEAH a big hug.)

LEAH: Oh my god, woman. You did so well. How do you feel??!

(Beat. Then)

SHANNON: Like a bad ass bitch.

6. A New Woman

(A couple of hours later. JOSH *is crashed out on the couch in front of the Twins' game on TV. We watch him for a couple of beats—long enough to witness a loud snore or two.)*

*(*SHANNON *enters in her same yoga outfit from the previous scene. She sees* JOSH *and just stops. She stares at him for a beat. She rubs her left ear.)*

(She tiptoes past him and he startles awake. Sees her)

JOSH: *(Groggy)* Hey.

SHANNON: Hey.

JOSH: You left your yoga mat.

SHANNON: Where are the kids?

JOSH: What time is it?

SHANNON: Where are the boys, Josh?

JOSH: At the party—I don't know—what time is—

SHANNON: You don't know?

JOSH: Sheila has them. She took pity on me and offered to take them home with her after the party for a playdate.

SHANNON: You left them with Sheila—

JOSH: And her nanny. Whatshername…

SHANNON: Katya.

JOSH: Yeah. They love her.

SHANNON: I know.

JOSH: They're fine.

SHANNON: She will hold this over me. I will not hear the end of her "generosity" for a very long time. And they'll come home all hopped up on sugar and carbs and—

JOSH: You're welcome. You're welcome for the extra time you have to yourself. I thought we could use some alone time in the middle of the day. I thought we could connect. You know. It's been a while and we're always so tired at night. Whatever. But I guess…

(This guilt bomb connects.)

SHANNON: Okay. I'm sorry. I just…

JOSH: They're fine.

(Beat)

(SHANNON rubs her left ear.)

JOSH: Hugo was being really sweet to Bear today.

SHANNON: Really?

JOSH: It was like a miracle. They were holding hands at one point walking through that place. That hell hole. Chuck E Fucking Cheese.

SHANNON: They were holding hands?

(JOSH pulls out his phone and SHANNON moves to him.)

JOSH: *(Handing her the phone)* Here.

(SHANNON snuggles into JOSH to see the pic.)

SHANNON: Oh my god. So cute.

JOSH: Yeah. It really was.

(SHANNON hands JOSH the phone.)

SHANNON: Thanks.

(JOSH puts the phone away.)

JOSH: How was yoga?

SHANNON: What? *(She rubs her left ear again.)*

JOSH: You okay? You keep rubbing your ear.

SHANNON: Oh. It's just…like a little plugged up. And buzzing.

JOSH: Weird.

SHANNON: It's nothing.

JOSH: You should take an Airborne or something. Might be a cold.

(SHANNON *looks at* JOSH.)

JOSH: What?

(SHANNON *kisses* JOSH.)

JOSH: That was nice.

(*Beat. Electricity flows powerfully between* SHANNON *and* JOSH.)

(SHANNON *kisses* JOSH *again. Hungrily. She pulls back and looks deeply into his eyes.*)

JOSH: Whoa.

(JOSH *kisses* SHANNON's *neck. He buries his face in her neck and inhales her. He pulls back. Confused for a second.*)

SHANNON: What?

JOSH: Nothing. (*Beat*) Incense?

SHANNON: What?

JOSH: Never mind.

(JOSH *kisses* SHANNON. *They need each other. They need this.*)

SHANNON: What time is Sheila bringing them back?

JOSH: Two o'clock.

SHANNON: We have time.

(SHANNON *climbs on top of* JOSH. *She pulls his shirt up over his head.*)

JOSH: Here? In the living room?

SHANNON: Oh yeah. I'm gonna fuck your brains out, baby.

(Lights)

(End of scene)

END OF ACT ONE

ACT TWO

7. Like Cheating

(The next day. Early morning. Lights up on LEAH *and* SHANNON *on their park bench clutching their coffee.* LEAH *is "wearing" her baby again.)*

SHANNON: Oh my God, Leah. I keep seeing it in my hand. *The gun.* And I'm like…yeah. That was me. I did that. And the bullseye. You saw that.

LEAH: Yep, I saw it.

SHANNON: My ear's still ringing, though. Does that ever happen to you?

LEAH: Mmm…no.

SHANNON: Uh oh.

LEAH: It's only been a day.

SHANNON: Should I be worried? I mean what if I like blew out an eardrum or something?

LEAH: If it still hurts tomorrow, maybe call your doctor. But, I think if you actually damaged something it would hurt a lot more.

SHANNON: Okay. I hope you're right.

LEAH: Don't worry.

SHANNON: *(To the kids)* I see you! That's a huge one! Wow!

LEAH: *(To the kids)* You kept trying and trying and you didn't give up and you did it.

SHANNON: *(To the kids)* You did it!

LEAH: *(To the kids)* Not now, baby. Just keep blowing those bubbles. The fairies need their breakfast.

SHANNON: *(To* LEAH*)* Stroke of genius bringing bubbles for the kids.

LEAH: Had 'em in the car for emergencies.

SHANNON: They're playing so well.

LEAH: For now. Let's enjoy it.

*(*SHANNON *and* LEAH *toast their coffee. They sip.)*

SHANNON: I feel like I'm cheating on Josh.

LEAH: Why?

SHANNON: I didn't tell him.

LEAH: Oh, Shannon.

SHANNON: I know. But I can't tell him. Not like this. I think I have to work up to it. Lay the groundwork so that he doesn't hate you and punish me—

LEAH: Punish you?

SHANNON: I mean like by just being an asshole.

LEAH: He's an asshole? He doesn't seem like an asshole.

SHANNON: No, just...I mean, he won't want me to be friends with you. And I have the right to be friends with whoever I want. Right? I mean, you don't just give up that right when you get married.

LEAH: No, but...I do not want to come between your marriage.

SHANNON: Just don't tell him. Please.

LEAH: I wouldn't tell him. But...

SHANNON: Because I'm serious. He would totally freak. The gun thing is big.

LEAH: Secrets in a marriage...they're like poison.

SHANNON: I can't tell him, Leah. I just can't.

LEAH: Okay.

SHANNON: I love my husband. But...he's...he can be... *inflexible.*

LEAH: Okay.

SHANNON: You never keep anything from Danny?

LEAH: Sometimes I masturbate when he's asleep. And then I feel guilty but only for a second because he wouldn't want me waking him up.

(SHANNON *laughs.*)

LEAH: Seriously, though. I would hate to be the cause of a rift in your marriage. I already feel guilty.

SHANNON: Don't feel guilty. You gave me a gift. You freed me from my fear. I never expected this. Never. And I can't even figure out completely what it was. The adrenaline rush, the complete possession of my body. This power. It infused me. And it has stayed with me. We walked out of the range and I didn't have to think about how to hold my body, I walked tall without a single thought. I went home and had the best sex of my marriage.

LEAH: Get the fuck out.

SHANNON: Seriously. It was...it was gooood. So it can't be bad, right? It's weird. But it's like something inside me has just calmed down. I don't know how else to explain it. Last night before dinner, Bear had to pee but didn't want to go to the bathroom. It's his power thing, you know. Usually I fight him. I've been known to carry him flailing and screaming to the toilet. I know. Awful. But last night, I didn't do that. When he said

no. I calmly said, okay. And yes, he peed his pants.
So I calmly changed him. I didn't shame him. I didn't
lecture him. I didn't feel that thing inside that pulls
me towards the anger. I was just in the moment. And
then twenty minutes later he went into the bathroom
alone, pulled his pants down by himself and peed in
the potty. It was a miracle. It's like because I finally felt
empowered, I didn't have to fight for power with Bear.
Does that make sense?

LEAH: That's really huge.

SHANNON: But, do you think it's kind of fucked up that
it took shooting a gun to finally feel powerful?

LEAH: It's not the gun that made you feel that way, it's
that you confronted a massive fear.

SHANNON: Okay. Yeah. That's better.

(Beat. SHANNON and LEAH drink their coffee. They watch
the kids. SHANNON rubs her ear.)

LEAH: Danny's taking a few hours off this afternoon so
I can go surfing. You should come.

SHANNON: Surfing?

LEAH: You gotta try it at least once.

SHANNON: I never even go in the water when I take the
kids to the beach.

LEAH: Are you serious?

SHANNON: I don't like the feeling of the salt water on
my skin. The sticky residue. And when it rains? Forget
it. The rain flushes all of Los Angeles out to sea. The
grime of the streets, the smog residue, the garbage- it
all gets flushed during a storm and pushed out to the
Santa Monica Bay. Bacteria levels end up off the charts.
You're not supposed to go in the water for three days
after a storm. Three days. Did you know that? Most
people don't know that. Medical waste washed up

on Dockweiler Beach one time- we're talking tampon applicators, hypodermic needles and condoms. Yeah. No thank you. Anything you flush ends up in the ocean. I mean, no. No, thank you. No. I'm not letting my kids swim in that either. We go North if we go to the beach at all. To Malibu. But we always check bacteria levels. And again, we wait at least a week after a storm. Because hepatitis is too high a price for a day at the beach, if you ask me. I mean seriously.

LEAH: You know, I've never gotten Hepititis or a Staph infection from surfing the Bay. And the kids haven't either and we go to the beach a lot. Even after a storm.

SHANNON: Well, you really shouldn't, Leah. That's just playing with fire. I have a friend from work who went surfing after a storm with a cut on his leg. He wore a wet suit and everything but the cut got infected with strep and he almost died. Literally.

LEAH: You're a new woman, now. Maybe this new woman wants to surf. You should ask her.

(Lights shift.)

(JOSH is sitting on the couch looking at his phone.)

(SHANNON leaves the bench and crosses to the couch. LEAH grabs her surfboard and paddles out to sea. She remains in the scene somehow- but in her own area...that is her ocean.)

SHANNON: *(To JOSH)* Then she grabbed her board like it was as light as a rice cake and charged the water. In seconds, she was paddling fearlessly out to sea. She looked so strong. And she made it look so easy. Like she belonged there. Like a mermaid. And I'm just watching her. I cannot take my eyes off of her. She stops paddling and waits for her wave. So peaceful. Like one with nature. You know?

JOSH: Mm.

SHANNON: And in that instant I was desperate to be
her on that board. Surrounded by water. Her wave
comes. How she knows it's her wave, I haven't a clue,
but she's paddling again. On a mission. The wave
reaches her and she pops up on her board like it's
nothing and she glides. She becomes the wave. She
isn't just surfing the wave. She IS the wave. And it's
gentle and it's beautiful and when she was done she
had this glow. She was buzzing with life. And without
thinking...I grab the other board. It was a lot heavier
than I expected.

JOSH: What?

SHANNON: I grabbed the other board.

JOSH: Okay.

SHANNON: I couldn't run with it like Leah. But I make
it to the water with the board and Leah looks kind of
shocked. I mean, I don't blame her. I'm shocked. I'm in
the ocean on a surf board and I don't know even know
what I'm doing. I'm not thinking. I'm just paddling.
I feel strong and terrified all at once. The water
splashing my face—

JOSH: Hang on. What?

SHANNON: Pay attention.

JOSH: You went in the water?

SHANNON: Yes. Before I know it, I'm floating. Being.
Just being. I've forgotten what that feels like to just be.
I'm always doing. Always running to the next thing.
Managing feelings— mine, my clients, the kids, yours.
Managing...curating moments. Negotiating fights,
contracts, clients...acquiring more to get more...more
listings to get more money to get more stuff to buy
more time to just be. But being never happens. *(Beat)*
Here I am in the ocean on a surf board—

JOSH: Metaphorically.

SHANNON: Is that a joke?

JOSH: No. I just…you really went surfing?

SHANNON: That's what I'm telling you. Are you even listening?

JOSH: Yeah. I mean…I am now.

SHANNON: Now I forgot what I was saying.

JOSH: You're in the ocean on a surf board.

SHANNON: I'm in the ocean on a surf board and I'm not thinking about bacteria or the decline of our democracy. I'm not thinking about how I need to make a thousand phone calls. Or how we need to find a preschool for Bear. I'm not worrying about how to make sure our boys grow up to be good people, not rapists. How I need to be doing so much more for the kids. How I'm never doing enough, never being enough…I'm just being. I feel the tightness in my chest release. I feel my heart pounding against my body. It's pounding so hard I can hear it. I hear the water and I'm not afraid. I'm just present. A wave comes and Leah starts yelling

LEAH: Go, go, go!

SHANNON: I start paddling. I don't know what the fuck I'm doing. But I'm paddling and I…I hear Leah over the sound of the ocean. She's yelling something…I can't make it out—

LEAH: Now!

SHANNON: But I grab my board and pop up out the water…I land on my board. Standing! My first try and for a split second…I'm flying.

LEAH: Wooooo hooooo!

JOSH: Then what?!

SHANNON: Oh, the wave creamed me. It completely
had its way with me . I was the ocean's chew toy.
I manage to get to shore and just collapse. I was
annihilated. Just drenched and sticky and my eyes
were burning, but I didn't care.

LEAH: *(To* SHANNON*)* You did it.

SHANNON: I did it.

(LEAH *exits with her board.)*

(A beat)

JOSH: This really happened?

SHANNON: Yes.

JOSH: To you?

SHANNON: I know. Doesn't sound like me.

JOSH: Nope. Not at all.

SHANNON: It was amazing, Josh. I feel like a new
woman! Ever since I met Leah—

JOSH: I don't like how easily you're changing for her.

SHANNON: I really thought you'd be proud of me. I
hoped you'd be proud of me.

JOSH: I've been trying to get you to go surfing with me
with me for years. Years. And Leah shows up and you
just…for her you'll go. For her you'll change. But not
for me.

SHANNON: It's not like that. She just asked me at the
right time. That's all. What are you so upset about?

JOSH: I'm not upset. Don't…don't tell me I'm upset
when I'm not upset. Don't put that emotion on me.
You hate it when I do that to you.

SHANNON: Okay, it's just / you *seem* upset.

JOSH: I'm not upset. I'm…sad. Okay? I'm sad.

SHANNON: You're sad.

JOSH: I wanted your first time to be with me.

(Beat. SHANNON goes to JOSH. But he's too sad [not upset] and he just can't so he exits…)

(End of scene)

8. Some Good Whiskey

(DANNY and JOSH sitting on JOSH's front porch drinking DANNY's homemade whiskey.)

JOSH: *(Regarding the whiskey)* That's tight.

DANNY: Yeah, dude. Glad you like it.

JOSH: That's some good whiskey. I'll give you that.

DANNY: You'll give me that?

JOSH: Never mind.

(Quiet. DANNY and JOSH sip the whiskey.)

DANNY: Digging this front porch situation. Old school.

JOSH: I like it.

DANNY: My old man used to sit in the garage in his lawn chair with a beer at the end of the day just watching the world around him.

JOSH: I come out here after getting the kids down for the night and just sit…think…sometimes sneak a cigarette.

DANNY: You put the kids to sleep?

JOSH: Depends on the day.

(Silence again. DANNY looks around for something else to comment on.)

DANNY: Had some of your avocados.

JOSH: Oh?

DANNY: Guess Shannon gave some to Leah.

JOSH: More than we can ever eat.

DANNY: Avocados in your backyard. Best thing about Southern California. That and the earthquakes.

JOSH: Funny.

DANNY: Seriously, I love earthquakes.

JOSH: There's something wrong with you.

DANNY: Yeah. Anyway, love avocados.

(JOSH *just looks at* DANNY. *He is not helping things. More silence, sipping whiskey, looking for something to talk about.*)

DANNY: Those new kicks?

JOSH: —

DANNY: Your Vans.

JOSH: You're asking me if my shoes are new?

DANNY: Dude, this wasn't my fucking idea. Leah wouldn't shut up about it.

JOSH: Well, you tried.

DANNY: Yeah.

JOSH: Your whiskey's good. I'll give you that.

DANNY: You can stop.

JOSH: Thanks for stopping by, neighbor. Would you like to take some avocados home with you? We also have a lemon tree. Can get you some of those too.

DANNY: Leah told me I can't come home until we work this out.

JOSH: Work this out?

DANNY: You could try a little harder, dude. I mean, fuck.

JOSH: So this is on me?

DANNY: I extended the olive branch.

(Off JOSH's *look:)*

DANNY: The whiskey.

JOSH: Guess I'll take some more.

(Beat. DANNY *pours* JOSH *more. They sip. Now okay with the silence.)*

JOSH: Am I tasting…bacon?

DANNY: Yeah. You taste it?

JOSH: I do.

DANNY: I used a bacon tincture.

JOSH: A bacon tincture?

DANNY: Shit, you're not vegetarian, are you?

JOSH: I ate steak at your house.

DANNY: Right. I forgot.

JOSH: Pretty damn good olive branch.

DANNY: Was hoping it would do some of the heavy lifting.

JOSH: Let me just ask you, Danny. What do you see as the outcome here?

DANNY: I don't know. Moving past it. The gun thing.

JOSH: Moving past it. Like we just…agree to disagree?

DANNY: Sure. It is possible, you know.

JOSH: It's always gonna be there. I'm always gonna know.

DANNY: You don't have any other friends who are gun owners?

JOSH: No.

DANNY: That you know.

JOSH: I do know.

DANNY: I was hoping you'd be cool.

JOSH: Sorry to disappoint.

DANNY: I was hoping you'd be open. I was hoping you'd be open to talking…without your preconceived notions. I thought that might be possible. Because I do like you. I mean…I did before you freaked out about me being a law-abiding responsible gun owner and—

JOSH: I admit I reacted strongly that night…. It was a shock.

DANNY: I get that.

JOSH: And then you got all John Wayne about being a gun owner and…you have the right, I guess whatever, to own guns…and I have the right to not associate with you.

DANNY: Are you really that fucking intolerant? *(Correcting himself)* Sorry. Don't you think maybe, perhaps, that might be the slightest bit…intolerant?

JOSH: You gun people are always talking about / your rights.

DANNY: Don't say "you gun people".

JOSH: It's always about your precious second amendment right. You get to feel safe by arming yourself. But what about the rest of us? What about my right to feel safe? How do I get to feel safe from you?

DANNY: From me?

JOSH: No not you. Not what I meant. Not you. The people with guns.

DANNY: Maybe if you owned a gun you would actually feel safe.

JOSH: So, that's it? Own a gun. That's the answer.

DANNY: Learn how to use it. Store it properly.

JOSH: Under my pillow? In bedside table?

DANNY: Yeah. In your bedside table. That's in every gun-owner's pamphlet. Don't be an asshole.

JOSH: I just don't buy into the argument that the only way to feel safe in America is to arm yourself.

DANNY: Then don't. But don't restrict the rest of us. Instead, try educating yourself. Re-think the issue. Guns aren't the problem.

JOSH: Right. Guns don't kill people…they only fire deadly projectiles at fatal velocities and if you happen to be in the path, you die.

DANNY: Ha. That's clever. But still wrong. Guns don't fire themselves.

JOSH: I have a right to feel the way I feel about guns.

DANNY: Maybe it would help if you told me why you're so emotional about—

JOSH: I know you mean that as a dig / but I'm okay being emotional about this.

DANNY: No, I don't.

JOSH: Yeah. I care. So I'm emotional. You say that more guns is the answer, but do realize that wielding a gun actually increases a person's bias to see guns in the hands of others? Being a gun owner actually makes you paranoid. That's a scientific fact. So, no I don't buy…and I will never buy that more guns are the answer.

DANNY: Speaking from experience, that's total bullshit.

JOSH: There's a study.

DANNY: Always a study. Any study can prove any point. Before I say this, I want you to remember…I'm a liberal. Okay. So listen with that filter— The right to bear arms…it's essential. Especially right fucking now. Do you really want only Trump supporters to have guns? The white supremacists? The fucking Nazis and the KKK?

(DANNY *gives that a beat to really land with* JOSH)

DANNY: Yeah. You should be glad there are people on our side packing heat.

(Beat. JOSH *actually considers this point.)*

JOSH: Okay. I see that. I do. But...isn't it better to go through life trusting that people are inherently good vs. out to get you?

DANNY: Are you serious? You're welcome to live in your fantasy land, but I gotta live in reality and I'm someone who likes to be prepared.

(A beat. DANNY *looks at* JOSH *and considers—he might have actually gotten through to him.)*

DANNY: You should come with me to the range.

JOSH: That's funny.

DANNY: Knowledge is power.

JOSH: Just thinking about it makes my skin crawl. And the more we talk about this, the more angry I'm getting.

DANNY: See, that's what I don't get. Why? What does my having a gun / have anything to do with you?

JOSH: Eleven guns.

DANNY: Shannon and Leah aren't gonna stop hanging out. You get that, right? They're like soul sisters or whatever. And dude, aside from this one issue, I thought you were a cool guy. I saw us hanging. Watching baseball...

JOSH: So I'm just supposed to compartmentalize this?

DANNY: I mean, yeah.

JOSH: I'm supposed to pretend you're not a gun guy.

DANNY: Dude, I'm not a "gun guy." I have guns. And I like to shoot them, yeah, but…

JOSH: You're a gun guy, man. You're a hipster gun guy.

DANNY: I am not a fucking hipster!

(DANNY *grabs the whiskey out of* JOSH's *hands.*)

JOSH: What the fuck?

DANNY: I'm not a hipster. Take it back.

JOSH: I guess it's possible I have the definition wrong…

(DANNY *hands the whiskey back to* JOSH.)

DANNY: Sorry. I…I don't like labels. And you don't know me. You've made all these assumptions about me and it really fucking pisses me off. I mean, have you ever even shot a gun?

JOSH: Yes.

DANNY: What kind?

JOSH: BB gun.

DANNY: I mean a real gun.

JOSH: Did you ever think that maybe this idea that you need to protect your family is a myth that's fed to you by the NRA so that you'll buy more guns?

DANNY: It's no myth, man. And have you seen this administration?

JOSH: Okay. For argument's sake. Say it comes to that. Say the government goes full fascist. Internment camps for minorities and political dissidents—

DANNY: "Say it comes to that?" It HAS come to that.

JOSH: No, I mean—

DANNY: You think I don't think about this every day?

JOSH: Of course—

DANNY: Yeah I do feel the need to protect myself as a man of color in America.

JOSH: I'm not saying you shouldn't but—

DANNY: But.

JOSH: Forget it.

DANNY: Nah, say it.

JOSH: No, I'm sorry. I'm…

DANNY: Say it. Your point. You were getting around to one.

JOSH: *(Beat)* Okay. You really think that you could face down the world's most powerful military with your garage arsenal?

DANNY: *(Beat. Considers this)* No. But…I wouldn't have to face the entire military all at once, would I? Maybe just a handful at a time and I'm a pretty good shot. Leah's even better. So, yeah…I feel solid. *(Beat. Change of tactic.)* What do you have? A Louisville Slugger under your bed?

JOSH: No. I don't lie awake worried about an intruder every night. Fantasizing about someone breaking in and all the ways I could kill them to protect my family.

DANNY: Must be nice.

JOSH: —

DANNY: Look—

JOSH: Listen—

DANNY: I'm only saying—

JOSH: I get what you're saying, I just—

DANNY: This is the problem with liberals—

JOSH: The problem with—

DANNY: Lectures, judgement. Never listening.

JOSH: What's wrong with a security system?

DANNY: Nothing.

JOSH: ADT? Ring? Sure. A gun? No.

DANNY: Again, my choice.

JOSH: Statistics aren't in your favor. And also- you said you keep your guns in the garage in a locked safe? So, how do you even get to them in time if you have an intruder?

DANNY: I have a handgun in a small, locked safe hidden in our bedroom.

JOSH: Ah, the whole picture.

DANNY: You teeing up a statistic?

JOSH: Nope. You seem to have heard it all.

DANNY: Pretty much.

JOSH: Guns are not dangerous, right? They're just bits of plastic and metal.

DANNY: Exactly.

JOSH: Designed for one purpose: to end life.

DANNY: I told Leah this wouldn't work. "Just talk to him," she said. Talk. Ha.

JOSH: Look, I know I'm uncompromising about this / but I'm okay with that.

DANNY: Ya think?

JOSH: I have to be on the side of humans over weapons. That's it. And I'm perfectly at peace with being unarmed.

DANNY: Aren't you sick of being outnumbered? Why should the racist, homophobic, women haters of this country be the only ones with the guns? Doesn't that scare the shit out of you? I mean, it does me. I want more people like us to own guns because I see what's happening in the world. I'm paying attention.

JOSH: Yeah, this isn't happening.

DANNY: Because you're incapable of actually talking about it. You're not able to talk like talk without judgement or jumping to conclusions or getting angry. You come to the conversation with anger. And why are you so mad at me, anyway?

JOSH: I—

DANNY: So I own guns. I'm not mad at you for *not* owning guns. Why are you mad at *me*? It's not like I'm out there killing people. I'm not advocating that a militia rise up. I'm not waving my gun around like it's an extension of my dick. Dude, for the record, there's nothing I hate more than irresponsible gun owners. I choose to protect my family with a gun and I respect the huge responsibility that comes with that. I do not take it lightly. I never would. So, I ask again. Why are you so fucking mad at me?

(Beat)

JOSH: I'm not.

DANNY: You fucking are.

JOSH: I'm trying not to be because I get how irrational that is, but I listen to you and…no. Forget it.

DANNY: We're doing this.

JOSH: Fine. You say you have a gun because you are exercising your right to protect your family. It makes you feel safer when research shows that having a gun in your home actually makes you less safe and more likely to be a victim of gun violence. But facts don't fucking matter, do they? You don't have guns because they actually make you safer, you have guns because they make you *feel* safer. And in your effort to feel safer, you've made me not only feel less safe, but you've made me, and yourself for that matter, *statistically* less safe.

DANNY: Not true.

JOSH: All these people buying guns to feel safer make the rest of us statistically less safe. It's true. There are studies. More guns do not make us more safe. Anything that says otherwise is just NRA propaganda.

DANNY: Statistics or not, we have the right to bear arms. Guns aren't going away. And maybe life would be easier if you just accepted that fact.

JOSH: This isn't gonna work. I'm here. You're there.

DANNY: I have guns and you hate me for it. You don't have guns and I could give two shits.

JOSH: So?

DANNY: Which one of us is the intolerant one?

JOSH: It's forced upon me. I have no say in the matter.

DANNY: You have a say. This is America. You get to have a gun or not have a gun. It's your say. Your choice. That's what's beautiful about this country.

(JOSH *dismayed just shakes his head.*)

DANNY: You want me to go? I'll go.

JOSH: I'm not intolerant.

DANNY: Okay.

JOSH: I'm not.

DANNY: It's a loaded issue…so to speak.

JOSH: Yeah.

DANNY: You want to talk about something else, we'll talk about something else.

(*Sip of whiskey*)

JOSH: You see Mauer's walk-off homer the other day?

DANNY: Heard about it.

JOSH: It was a thing of beauty.

DANNY: He had a pretty bad April.

JOSH: Abhorrent.

DANNY: Good for him for pulling himself up out of that.

JOSH: Hoping it sticks.

DANNY: Say the word and I'll get us tickets for when they're in town.

JOSH: Man...I don't know.

DANNY: Just baseball.

JOSH: True.

(DANNY *and* JOSH *sip their whiskey and settle for a beat or two.*)

DANNY: But seriously, I really think if you just came with me to the range—

JOSH: No.

DANNY: Just once. You'll see.

JOSH: I don't need to fire a gun to know how I feel about them.

DANNY: Come on.

JOSH: I'm never saying yes.

DANNY: You'll love it.

JOSH: No. And I won't. And stop asking.

DANNY: Your wife did.

(*A long fucking beat.*)

(*Oh fuck*)

JOSH: What did you just say to me?

DANNY: Your wife went with Leah to the range. You didn't know?

(No response)

DANNY: Oh man. I thought you knew. Leah said she was amazing. Like just took to it immediately and … you know they say that women are better shooters than men? And…

(JOSH stands up.)

JOSH: Thanks for the whiskey. *(He turns to head back into the house.)*

DANNY: You okay, man?

JOSH: Get off my fucking porch.

(End of scene)

9. The Confrontation

(A couple of hours later. JOSH sits at the kitchen table at his laptop drinking whiskey. Sound of the front door off. He closes his laptop. He looks up. Waits)

(SHANNON enters carrying a bag of groceries. She's wearing a business casual dress.)

(She is in a good mood. She enters and immediately starts putting away the groceries through the following.)

SHANNON: I got the listing! It's official. Guess what price we settled on.

(Beat. No response)

SHANNON: Three point three million. Three. Point. Three. MILLION. And there's more! I have a dual offer on the Grandview house. *(She looks at JOSH)* Babe? *(Beat)* Did you hear me?

JOSH: I thought I smelled something. Thought you might have snuck a cigarette or something.

SHANNON: What?

JOSH: But that wasn't it.

SHANNON: What are you talking about?

JOSH: You lied to me.

SHANNON: I don't know what you're talking about.

JOSH: You fucking lied.

SHANNON: Are you drunk?

JOSH: Yoga. You went to yoga with Leah. How many times? Just that once?

SHANNON: I'm not talking to you while you're drunk.

JOSH: That day you went to yoga. You came home and fucked me like you haven't fucked me in years so I didn't say anything about you smelling slightly like... smoke or...what I never would have fathomed at the time...gunpowder.

SHANNON: Josh...

JOSH: You lied right to my face.

SHANNON: I didn't lie...I just didn't tell you.

JOSH: So it's true. You went to the driving range with Leah.

SHANNON: Shooting range.

JOSH: What?

SHANNON: You said driving range. That's golf. Doesn't matter.

JOSH: Are you fucking serious, right now?

SHANNON: Let me...

JOSH: Let you talk?

SHANNON: That'd be nice.

JOSH: What the fuck, Shannon? I thought we were a team. I thought we were on the same side. I thought I knew you.

SHANNON: If you'd just listen—

JOSH: You don't just go from "take away all the guns" to "from my cold dead hands" over fucking night!

SHANNON: You're being dramatic.

JOSH: You held a gun, pointed it at a target and shot it.

SHANNON: A lot of people do that, Josh. You realize.

JOSH: Not you. Not you. Not my wife.

SHANNON: I made a choice. I'm a grown woman. And I made a choice, Josh.

JOSH: I knew Leah was bad news the second I met her.

SHANNON: You did not.

JOSH: Before you met her, you'd never have even considered looking at a gun, let alone touching it. She's a bad influence!

SHANNON: What's so bad?

JOSH: What's so bad?

SHANNON: Yeah, what's so bad about me knowing how to fire a gun?

JOSH: We're not gun people.

SHANNON: At least one of us knows how to fire a gun if we ever need to defend ourselves.

JOSH: Who are you?

SHANNON: I'm still me, Josh.
I'm just...

JOSH: What?

SHANNON: Empowered.

JOSH: Holy fucking shit. Holy fucking shit.

SHANNON: You're gonna wake the kids.

JOSH: So you're empowered now, huh? What the hell were you before?

SHANNON: Scared. All the time. About everything.

JOSH: Okay, okay, okay, okay, so…what, so now… what…

SHANNON: I was. And don't tell me I wasn't because you don't know. You don't know what it's like to be a woman in this world. I can't even do my job without making sure I have back up. Can't meet a client alone. Can't sit an open house alone. Can't ever walk into a room before my client. Always having to be the one to make sure I don't end up a victim. And I never considered a gun an option because I was afraid of them too. So scared of even the idea of a gun. And why? Why was I so scared? My fear of guns wasn't healthy. And I've conquered it. I've conquered my fear, Josh. This is a good thing. It feels good. I don't know how to explain it but…it unlocked something in me. And I'm…I know this is gonna sound really…I don't know…but this listing…biggest listing of my career…I wouldn't have gotten it before.

JOSH: Before firing a gun? Firing a gun got you this listing?
You seriously believe that?!

SHANNON: Let's not pretend that I was like the most confident person in the room, Josh. We are both very familiar with my anxiety issues.

JOSH: So they're just magically gone now because you went to the range with Leah?

SHANNON: Pretty much.

JOSH: How many times?

(SHANNON *doesn't answer.*)

JOSH: How many times have you gone to a shooting range with Leah?

SHANNON: A few.

JOSH: Did you go with her tonight? To celebrate getting your listing?

SHANNON: No. I went to a class.

JOSH: A class? What kind of—

SHANNON: A gun safety class.

(JOSH *stands.*)

JOSH: That's not happening.

SHANNON: Josh…I really think if we talk about this when things calm down, that you might be able to understand—

JOSH: You're empowered now? You weren't empowered before?

SHANNON: I can't talk to you when you're like this.

JOSH: You need a gun to feel strong, is that it?

SHANNON: Babe…is this really about guns or is this something else? Because this feels like something else. Like something deeper.

JOSH: Don't do that.

SHANNON: You're so mad and I'm trying really hard to stay calm right now, but I really don't like the way you're talking to me.

JOSH: How would you feel if suddenly I became obsessed with…I don't know…meth.

SHANNON: Meth?!

JOSH: And I kept it from you. You kept this from me because you knew it was wrong. What you're doing. You know it's wrong. You can't even look at yourself in the mirror, I bet.

SHANNON: I have no problem with that, thanks for caring.

JOSH: I feel like I'm losing my wife.

(SHANNON *laughs.*)

SHANNON: *(Off his look)* I'm sorry.

JOSH: Don't fucking laugh at me.

SHANNON: I'm sorry.

JOSH: We've always agreed on all the big issues. Always.

SHANNON: I know. Which is why I didn't want to like shooting that gun. I really didn't want to. But instead of feeling repulsion, I felt exhilaration. I felt strong. And why shouldn't I get to feel that way? When do I get to feel strong?

JOSH: You are strong.

SHANNON: With you I feel strong. You've always made me feel safe. But when you're not with me, the fear returns. Which means that I'm expecting you to protect me. And how selfish is that? To expect you to take care of my own personal protection? How weak is that?

JOSH: What the fuck are you talking about? Are you serious right now?

SHANNON: You love saying you're a feminist. But true feminism is about women having the opportunity to make choices. About everything. Including how we protect ourselves.

JOSH: Holy shit you've been brainwashed.

SHANNON: Josh.

JOSH: You've been totally fucking brainwashed. It's like invasion of the body snatchers. What have you done with my wife?! I want my wife back. Because I don't know who the fuck you are.

SHANNON: To suggest I've been brainwashed implies I'm easily manipulated and weak.

(JOSH *just looks at* SHANNON.)

SHANNON: So that's it. That's how you feel about me?

JOSH: I don't like how you've been changing for her. And it's not healthy. This obsession with Leah.

SHANNON: I'm not obsessed with her.

JOSH: You don't just wake up one day and decide to abandon all your principles for no reason.

SHANNON: I didn't abandon all my principles. I started thinking for myself. And all I did was fire a gun, Josh…

JOSH: No. If that's all it was- that you fired a gun and that's it - this wouldn't be such a big deal. But you just confessed to going to a class! Next you'll be telling me you want to buy a gun. That you're gonna join the NRA—

SHANNON: You're being ridiculous.

(JOSH *throws his glass and it shatters. A high pitched scream escapes* SHANNON. *A beat*)

(*They listen to make sure the kids didn't wake up.*)

(*Silence*)

(*A beat*)

JOSH: You're gonna call Leah and tell her that you can't see each other again. You're going to ask for your money back for that gun class and you're never going to go to a shooting range again.

(*Beat. Beat. Beat*)

JOSH: Understood?!

SHANNON: You're enraged because you can't control me anymore.

JOSH: I don't want to control you. I just want things back the way they were before.

SHANNON: When I agreed with you on everything?

JOSH: When you didn't lie to me.

SHANNON: And I agreed with you on everything?

JOSH: Sure. Sounds good. Let's go back to that.

SHANNON: Well, that's not happening. Because I'm my own person. And I have the right to think for myself. And if I want to fire a gun, I'll fire a gun. If I want to own a gun, I'll own a fucking gun... *(She points her finger in his face.)* Because you don't control me. Asshole.

(Without thinking, JOSH *grabs* SHANNON's *wrist. Tight)*

SHANNON: Ow!

*(*JOSH *holds* SHANNON *there like he's holding onto his life. He looks fucking scary.)*

SHANNON: Let me go!

*(*JOSH *doesn't let go. He also doesn't know what he's doing. Where this came from. And now that it's happened, now what...?)*

SHANNON: Josh! What the fuck?! You're hurting me! Let go!

*(*SHANNON *looks at* JOSH. *Makes eye contact. He releases her and takes a step back. He looks a little shaken and confused. She backs away from him holding her wrist.)*

(Beat)

SHANNON: What the fuck, Josh?!

(Beat)

JOSH: No more guns, Shannon. I mean it. *(He exits.)*

(A beat)

(SHANNON *looks at the mess on the floor. She goes to it. She begins to clean it up, picking up the larger shards of glass first. She pricks her finger and flinches. She sucks on it. A surge of emotion takes her by surprise. She shoves it back inside and continues to clean up* JOSH's *mess.*)

10. Tomatoes

(LEAH *is pruning her potted tomato plant in her front yard. She's wearing overalls.*)

(JOSH *enters in his business casual attire.*)

JOSH: Hey, neighbor.

LEAH: Hey, Josh.

JOSH: Doing some gardening?

LEAH: Yep.

JOSH: That a tomato plant?

LEAH: Yes it is. Organic Sun Gold. Try one.

(LEAH *hands* JOSH *a small yellow tomato from the plant. He tries it.*)

JOSH: Wow, so sweet.

LEAH: *(Handing him a basket of tomatoes)* Here. We have plenty. The kids love them.

JOSH: Thanks.

LEAH: No sweat. So…you on your lunch break or something?

JOSH: Thought I'd take Shannon out to lunch. Grab some ramen.

LEAH: Oh. That's sweet.

JOSH: Have you seen her?

LEAH: No.

JOSH: No?

LEAH: I haven't seen her. No.

JOSH: Okay. So she's not here.

LEAH: Everything okay?

JOSH: I just got fired.

LEAH: Oh no. Really?

JOSH: Yeah. I was not expecting that.

LEAH: I'm so sorry.

JOSH: I hate my job.

LEAH: Yeah. Shannon told me.

JOSH: She did?

LEAH: Just that she was hoping to make enough money in real estate so that you could quit and build that app you've been wanting to build. Guess you have the chance to do that now.

JOSH: Yeah. Guess I do.

LEAH: Still. That sucks. You guys should come over for dinner tonight.

JOSH: Have you talked to her at all today?

LEAH: To Shannon?

JOSH: Yeah. To Shannon. Your new best friend.

LEAH: I know the gun thing is um...

JOSH: Fucked up.

LEAH: Well, maybe. But...I just feel in my heart that it's worth it to work through it together. We are capable of working through this. I believe that. And I understand your reservations. I do.

JOSH: You do?

LEAH: I do.

JOSH: My reservations.

LEAH: Yes.

JOSH: You understand them.

LEAH: I think so.

JOSH: What are they, Leah? My reservations.

LEAH: You're worried that you're losing your wife.

JOSH: And why would I be worried about losing my wife?

LEAH: Because she's discovered her strength. And you're worried that means she doesn't need you anymore. But that's not true.

JOSH: I've always seen her strength. She's always been strong. That's why I fell in love with her. It's not something new. She hasn't just discovered suddenly that she's strong. She's always been strong.

LEAH: I didn't mean to imply—

JOSH: That you helped her discover this newfound strength?

LEAH: What I'm seeing is a freedom in her that—

JOSH: So she wasn't free before she met you either?

LEAH: Josh.

JOSH: She needed you to put a gun in her hand to make her feel both strong and free? That's what you're saying?

LEAH: She was afraid. All the time. And you know it. Shannon confronted a massive fear and discovered a well of strength she didn't know she even had. It's not about the gun. It's about confronting the fear. And with all due respect, you're a man so you don't have a clue what it's like to be a woman in the world. Fear is the skin sewn onto our bodies when we're born. You might not like the fact that your wife is growing out of her fear because of what that brings up in you.

JOSH: I find it remarkable that you have so much insight into our problems. You've just got it all figured out.

LEAH: I don't have it all figured out, but I'm not going to pretend I don't see things. And I'm suggesting that, yeah, maybe the gun isn't the problem at all. It might be useful for you to look at why you're so triggered by your wife's empowerment.

JOSH: The moment you put that gun in her hand, things began to change.

LEAH: Change is hard. For all of us.

JOSH: I don't recognize her.

LEAH: You don't recognize her.

JOSH: Nope.

LEAH: And you feel like she's growing apart from you?

(JOSH *just looks at* LEAH.)

LEAH: That must be hard for you.

JOSH: Yeah. Yeah. It is. It's hard. It's really really hard.

LEAH: Really hard.

JOSH: I know what you're doing.

LEAH: You know what I'm doing.

JOSH: Repeating everything I say. Shannon does that with the kids now when they're upset. Did you teach her that too?

LEAH: Shannon is an amazing woman, Josh. And she loves you so much. You have to know that.

JOSH: I don't need you to tell me anything about my wife. What I need is for you to stop brainwashing her.

Could you do that? Do you think you could maybe just find someone else to brainwash and leave her alone?

LEAH: You feel that I'm brainwashing her.

JOSH: Stop doing that.

LEAH: I'm listening. I want you know I hear you.

JOSH: It's pissing me off.

LEAH: Fine. You think I'm brainwashing your wife. What does that say about your opinion of her? That she's capable of being brainwashed?

JOSH: No, no, no. You don't get to turn this around on me. You show up in our lives and you bring your guns and your new age thinking and I've read the NRA propaganda. I've read the message boards on those gun toting websites. It's all about converting the anti-gunners. Just take one to the range and show them. Show them how guns aren't evil. Teach them about guns. Introduce them to the world of Second Amendment. Convert. Convert. Convert. You might have converted my wife, but you will not convert me. And I'm gonna do everything in my power to deprogram my wife. Because this shit…this is done.

LEAH: Well, sounds like you've got a plan.

JOSH: I do.

LEAH: Josh…I don't really know you. But I think you have a good heart. I believe you want to do the right thing. That's what motivates you. You're a great dad. You work really hard for your family.

JOSH: Just shut the fuck up!

LEAH: Shannon's a grown ass woman who thinks for herself and that threatens you, doesn't it? Scares the shit out of you.

JOSH: I am a feminist!

LEAH: I'm sure you think you are.

(DANNY *enters "wearing" the baby.*)

DANNY: Everything okay out here?

(LEAH *looks at* JOSH. DANNY *doesn't take his eyes off* JOSH.)

JOSH: Hey, Danny.

DANNY: Heard some yelling.

JOSH: Sorry 'bout that.

LEAH: Josh got fired today.

DANNY: Did he?

(*Beat*)

JOSH: Well, I'm gonna…

LEAH: Josh, for the record, I don't think you're a bad guy.

(JOSH *puts the basket of tomatoes on the ground.*)

JOSH: Tomatoes give Hugo heartburn.

(DANNY *and* LEAH *watch* JOSH *leave. End of scene*)

11. Intervention

(JOSH *is deep cleaning the kitchen. He stops to take a sip of his beer. Sound of the garage door. He chugs his beer. Places the empty on the counter*)

(SHANNON *enters carrying a large shoulder bag.*)

JOSH: You're home!

SHANNON: You're cleaning.

JOSH: Yes. Deep cleaning. Just wanted it to be clean for you when you got home. You've been gone all day.

SHANNON: I was negotiating a contract all day on the Grandview house.

JOSH: Oh, right. Did it go well?

SHANNON: We have an accepted offer. Ten thousand over asking. Thirty-day escrow.

JOSH: That's great. That's really great.

SHANNON: Yeah, it really is.

JOSH: Congratulations!

SHANNON: Thanks.

JOSH: Are you hungry? I made lasagna. Should be ready any minute.

SHANNON: I'm not hungry.

(Beat)

JOSH: Shan…

SHANNON: We need to talk, Josh.

JOSH: I know. About last night…

SHANNON: Where are the kids?

JOSH: They're at my sister's.

SHANNON: Your sister's?!

JOSH: For a sleepover.

SHANNON: Why?

JOSH: So we could have some alone time.

(SHANNON *notices the beer on the counter.*)

SHANNON: You're drinking alone?

JOSH: Just a beer.

SHANNON: I'm surprised you're drinking after last night.

JOSH: About last night…
Shan, I…I, I'm so ashamed. I don't know what came over me. I just…I lost it. I should never have grabbed your wrist like that. I don't know what happened…

(SHANNON *holds out her arm to show* JOSH *her wrist. He's horrified by what he sees.*)

JOSH: Oh, baby. I'm so sorry...Please forgive me. I'm so sorry.

SHANNON: I know you're sorry.

JOSH: The whiskey was a terrible idea.

SHANNON: So it's the whiskey's fault you smashed a glass and grabbed my wrist so hard it's black and blue?

JOSH: No. I didn't realize...I mean you're right. It was unacceptable and it will never happen again.

SHANNON: Josh—

JOSH: Never. I promise. I promise you.

SHANNON: I want to believe you.

JOSH: You know me, Shan. We've been through so much together. I love you so much. I love our life together and I would never do anything to jeopardize that. The way I behaved...that was not okay. I know that. And that's why I called a therapist today. I have an appointment next week. I don't know where that came from, but I'm gonna find out and I'm going to work on it to make sure it never happens again.

SHANNON: *(Measured)* Good.

JOSH: Because that's not me. You know me. That is not me. I don't know who that was.

SHANNON: I don't either.

JOSH: I don't want you to be scared of me. The way you're looking at me now...it breaks my heart.

SHANNON: You scared me.

JOSH: I know.

SHANNON: You took away my safe place.

JOSH: I'm so sorry.

SHANNON: You treated me like...like I was yours to control.

JOSH: I said I'm sorry.

SHANNON: Like I was your property.

JOSH: I said I'm getting help.

SHANNON: Like you didn't care if you hurt me.

JOSH: That's not true—

SHANNON: It's my turn to talk now.

JOSH: I wasn't done. I had this whole other thing I wanted to say.

SHANNON: See, you're doing it now. You don't even see how much you try to control me.

JOSH: I hear you.

SHANNON: Do you?

JOSH: You're saying I try to control you.

SHANNON: Because you do.

JOSH: I never should have grabbed your wrist like that. But in my defense, you've been keeping a huge secret from me. And no, I'm not saying that justifies how I reacted, but...I mean, if you'd never lied to me...

(Beat. SHANNON *considers how to respond...)*

SHANNON: I shouldn't have lied. You're right.

JOSH: Thank you.

SHANNON: It won't happen again.

JOSH: Okay.
So the other thing I wanted to say is about this whole gun thing.

SHANNON: I want to talk to you about that too.

JOSH: I prepared a slideshow—

(JOSH presses a button on his smart phone or tells
Alexa or whatever to start the slideshow. First slide
projects onto the wall is this statistic with an image:
*The CDC reports 33,736 people die each year from gun
shots.*)

JOSH: The CDC reports 33,736 people die each year
from gun shots.

SHANNON: Josh—

JOSH: 33,736 people each year, Shannon.

SHANNON: I know the statistics.

(Next slide:)

JOSH: *Last week in Woodstock, Illinois a toddler shot himself
in the mouth after finding his mom's gun on top of a cabinet.*
A toddler. His parents said they have no idea how he
got the gun because they always keep it on top of the
cabinet and thought it was safe.

SHANNON: Well, they're fucking idiots.

(Next slide:)

JOSH: *A man accidentally shoots his own hand at a gun
range in Reno, Nevada.*
And this guy who shot his own hand…it wasn't his
first time shooting a gun. He was a regular at this
range.

SHANNON: You need to let me talk because I have
something to tell you.

(Next slide:)

JOSH: *A good guy with a gun in a Wal-Mart parking lot
took it upon himself to intervene in a robbery-in-progress
and wound up shooting an innocent bystander who was just
unloading her shopping cart.*

(SHANNON *stands up.*)

JOSH: If you just see this…. If you just listen, I know—

SHANNON: You know I'll what? I'll change my mind?

JOSH: Yes! Because you're a reasonable woman.

SHANNON: You know I'm starting to worry that you have a serious problem. I'm glad you made that appointment with the therapist, Josh, because this fixation you have is not healthy. Your obsession—

JOSH: I'm not the one who's obsessed!

SHANNON: I like shooting guns. So fucking what.

JOSH: I can't believe you.

SHANNON: I can't believe YOU.

(Next slide:)

JOSH: *When you fire a gun, your body produces endorphins which produce a calm and relaxed feeling and a high-like sensation. The more you fire a gun, the more your body craves that feeling.*
Did you know this? That you can become physically addicted to firing a gun? Did you know that? Because you really should know that.

SHANNON: All I want to do is go take a bath and enjoy the fact that I negotiated the biggest contract of my career today.

JOSH: After this you can go take your bath.

SHANNON: The more you tell me what to do, the more I want to resist you.

JOSH: Shannon! SIT. DOWN.

(This scares SHANNON.)

(She sits.)

(Next slide:)

JOSH: *States with more gun owners also have higher suicide rates.*
That one's obvious.

(Next slide:)

JOSH: *Domestic abuse is five times more likely to turn deadly if a firearm is present in the home.*

SHANNON: Is that a threat or something?

JOSH: What? No! Wait. You think I'm abusive? Because I grabbed your wrist?

SHANNON: The second you grabbed my wrist and I saw the look in your eye, I knew.

JOSH: What?

SHANNON: That we could never come back from that.

JOSH: Are you serious? You completely terrorize this family with your newfound love of firearms... you go from being an anti-gun advocate to a fucking ammosexual over night and I'm the bad guy because, what? Because I held your wrist a little too tightly? I mean, come on. You milked that for all it was worth. "You bruised me, Josh." "You scared me, Josh." Give me a fucking break. YOU'RE the bad guy. Not me.

(SHANNON stands and starts to exit.)

JOSH: Wait, wait, wait, Shannon. I'm sorry. I'm sorry. This whole thing! Please stay. Please. I feel like I'm going crazy—

SHANNON: Last night after you passed out, I started to pack a bag. I packed bags for the kids. We were gonna be gone by the morning. Because I swore I would never give my husband a second chance to lay a hand on me. But then...I crawled into bed with the kids and I fell asleep. When I woke up, my mind was running a different tape. It was playing the favorites. Our favorites. You and me. I kept seeing you with the kids. And me. And my mind was working over time to convince me that what happened the night before was nothing. Nothing happened. It didn't happen. We can go back. We can just go back. *(Beat)* I know you'd never hurt the kids, Josh. But the problem is that I don't trust us anymore.

JOSH: We'll go to therapy. Together.

SHANNON: It's too late.

JOSH: It's not too late.

SHANNON: It's too late. I can't unsee that look in your eyes. I thought I could. All day I hoped I could. I hoped that when I got home I'd look at you and all would be forgiven and there'd be nothing between us but love. But…I see you now. I see you. And I don't like what I see.

JOSH: Shannon…

(SHANNON goes to exit. JOSH blocks her exit.)

SHANNON: Please move.

JOSH: You can't do this.

SHANNON: Josh.

JOSH: Please just listen.

SHANNON: Move. Josh.

(JOSH doesn't. SHANNON tries to dodge him, but he is faster and blocks her again. Not touching her, but blocking her.)

(She runs to the other side of the room and he follows to block her exit there.)

SHANNON: MOVE!

(JOSH doesn't. She dodges again and runs and trips and falls. The contents of her bag spill.)

(JOSH sees it first. The gun. It's in its case.)

JOSH: What the fuck is that? Is that a gun? You have a fucking gun?!

(SHANNON goes for it and grabs it. She holds it to her chest. JOSH backs away.)

JOSH: You brought a gun into our home. AWithout talking to me? Without a fucking care for me or our kids? Holy shit! Who the fuck do you think you are?!

(SHANNON *opens the case and takes the gun out.*)

JOSH: You better get the fuck out of here with that thing, you crazy bitch!

(SHANNON *starts loading the gun.*)

JOSH: You're loading it? Are you seriously fucking loading it right now?

SHANNON: You're scaring me, Josh. You're scaring me!

JOSH: You're the one with the gun and I'm scaring you?

SHANNON: You were gonna kill me. I saw it in your eyes.

JOSH: I've never hit you and I never would. I held your wrist.... That's all! I feel like everything is fucking crazy out of control and you...holy shit...you really fucking went and bought a gun!

SHANNON: Because of you. Because of you, Josh!

JOSH: Do you hear yourself? I'm the one who needs therapy? Me? Go ahead. Load your gun. I'm going to my sister's, getting the kids and getting the fuck away from you.

SHANNON: You can't do that.

JOSH: STOP LOADING THE FUCKING GUN!

(JOSH *grabs the gun right out of* SHANNON's *hand. It happens easily and in a split second. One second she has the gun, the next, he has it.*)

(*He looks at the gun in his hand.*)

JOSH: Just bits of plastic and steel?

SHANNON: Josh...

JOSH: It's so small.

SHANNON: Please.

JOSH: I've never held one before.

SHANNON: Please.

JOSH: *(Still looking at the gun)* How does this end, Shannon?

SHANNON: We'll go to therapy. Together. We'll go to therapy and work this out together. Both of us. Please. Just...put...

JOSH: *(Looking out)* How does this end?

SHANNON: *(Pleading)* I'm sorry...

JOSH: *(Important: this is not a goodbye)* I love you, Shannon.

(He should NEVER point the gun or even hold it like a gun. It should only ever rest in the palm of his hand.)

SHANNON: Please, Josh!

JOSH: I love you.

(Lights)

END OF PLAY